Psalms & Songs of Scripture

The Faith We Hold

BIBLE HYMNS OF FAITH

**OLD AND NEW TESTAMENT PSALMS AND SONGS
PREPARED FOR PERSONAL REFLECTION,
AND AS HYMNS FOR PUBLIC WORSHIP**

LUCILLE L. TURFREY

Paperback: 978-1-960861-69-6
eBook: 978-1-960861-70-2
Library of Congress Control Number: 2023917907

The author here acknowledges the expertise and ever-ready assistance throughout this project, of Mavis Smith whose musical knowledge far exceeds that of the author. I am very grateful for every assistance given.

The stained-glass window design on the cover, all photographs, art, poetry, and Scripture quotations—a personal paraphrase—are by the author.

Some songs appearing in the section titled Minor Prophets, also in the New Testament, are modified extractions from the author's prior anthology titled "FAITH ALIVE—RHYTHMS OF SCRIPTURE", and used by permission.

SWEETSPIRE LITERATURE
—— MANAGEMENT ——

CONTENTS

INTRODUCTION

The Old Testament Psalms are the songs of Israel, the Hebrew people. The Bible gives its Psalms to the whole world where they have become known and loved by countless millions. Some Psalms have been imprinted on the heart and sung with joy in the Church and at home. These have been translated, then paraphrased into the rhyme and rhythms that allow our choirs to voice their testimonies in song—for example: Psalm 23, beloved and sung from the depths of the soul! The ancient words become today's expression of praise!

The Old Testament abounds in poetry, at times covered by the prosaic text. This book offers many possible "hidden songs" of Scripture where the story-line engages the soul to rejoice in the spiritual truth it conveys. Here, a song may emerge from the prose as it reflects our own soul's journey—we have learned something more of God's faithfulness: it is time to express our faith by a song. This book opens the way for **Scripture in Song** to be sung in public worship or silently in the depths of the soul!

Let us observe afresh the content of Genesis, chapter 1—2:3. These words have been taken by faithful Biblical students through the centuries to give all but undeniable evidence that the Earth was created in six days. 'It was: the Bible tells us so!' However, what is the form of language utilised in this, the initial "news" of Scripture? What does this "report" really say to us?

The age-old transcript, handed down from the ancient Hebrew format, displays, I suggest—in classical mode—a spectacular poem set in the style of Repetition (just 1 of 7 major types). Observe: *The evening and the morning were the first day... the second day... the third day...* and so on. No rhyme, no rhythm—the Hebrew mode—yet perfect in the style selected by which to give a truly magnificent, superbly succinct, and thoroughly scientific rendition of the creation of the universe!

When set in poetic terms, a "day" can mean many things. And, have we not proclaimed—when observing an unacceptable event—'such a thing would never have happened *in my day!!!*'? How long was that day—24 hours, a season or, years perhaps? The term "day" is frequently used in Scripture (particularly via the Psalms in the poetic mode), to denote an era of time—a period not necessarily of 24 hours' duration. Observe:

The LORD hear thee in the day of trouble. Psalm 20:1.
Thy people shall be willing in the day of Thy power. Psalm 110:3.
The LORD scorns the wicked, He sees that His day is coming. Ps 37:13.

If we may take **poetic licence** when considering the "days" of creation, it will be noted that it takes time for fish to emerge and grow to maturity, time for seeds to germinate, time for trees to grow, time for the blossom to develop into fruit, time for the newly born to find its feet, flex its muscles, grow to full height and maturity. It is therefore logical to assume that the Creation of the Universe required, perhaps, **"a week of ages"**!

SEVEN HEBRAIC POETIC STYLES

Agreement
The following statement is in accord with the first. e.g. Psalm 24
Antithesis
The following statement states an opposing view.   "   Psalm 1
Acrostic
A psalm of 22 verses, set from the Hebrew alphabet   " Psalm 25
Paraphrase
Repetition of the statement using different words   " Psalm 29
Progression
Proceeding to a further thought on the subject   " Psalm 20
Question and Answer
Ask the question, provide the answer   " Psalm 24
Repetition
Repeating the same thought.   " Psalm 150

PART ONE

OLD TESTAMENT HISTORY

BIBLICAL HISTORY IN POETRY

Commencing with the Creation Poem, the Psalms of Scriptural History—selected because of their Hebraic poetical setting—will be augmented by many songs that have emerged in light of the text becoming so profoundly meaningful that it all but becomes a Hymn of Praise, or of Contemplation, of Prayer—Petition, Intercession, Dedication. In these songs, the prose becomes a poem! Such will be the **Psalms & Songs** of Part One:

SCRIPTURE IN SONG

The first "Good News" recorded regarding the **creation** of the Universe, clearly shows that there were but THREE creations—the Hebrew word *bara* states this unequivocally! The first creation occurred *BEFORE* "the first day"– this was the creation of **MATTER**! It is not until the fifth day that *bara* is used again: the creation of life—**MOTIVATION**. Then, on the sixth day, *bara* is employed 3 times to emphasise the creation of soul—**MEANING**. With the creation of humanity, we find irrefutable evidence of a "trinity" of being: body, mind, and soul! Genesis 1 may be seen as a Hebraic poem and, in this genre, a "day" may describe a long period of time. The words in **bold** print bring further emphasis to a "trinity" of being via *bara* in Songs 1 and 2.

1. IN THE BEGINNING
Genesis 1. Tune: *O for a heart* — 10.10.10.10.

Creation's flame has pierced the darkest night
And light begins her trek across all space;
The *universe* God built has set its course—
The evenings and the mornings signed Earth's days.

Creation's gift of *life* shaped myriad forms!
Abundant life found freedom in the seas.
Then birds soared high in song and built their nests:
The evenings and the mornings sealed their days.

A massive, great event, brought forth on Earth
The creatures of the land. And then God says:
'Let humankind now walk the Earth and know,
At evening and each morn, I'll guide their days.'

Creation's wondrous gift to Earth is life,
But we commune with God—our prayers we raise.
Rejoice! God gifted humans with our *soul*:
May evening and the morning echo praise!

Created in the likeness of the LORD?
Like Him? The soul is God's great gift to us—
We're formed from matter, mind, and meaning: THREE!
O Son, and Father, Spirit: guide our days!

THE PSALM OF CREATION

The 1st chapter of **GENESIS** may be read as a **Hebrew Poem of Repetition** and here paraphrased as a Psalm of praise. Take note: Genesis 1 states clearly that there were just 3 creations: Matter ... Life ... Humanity!

2. CREATION'S DAY

Genesis 1 – 2:3. Tune: *Beethoven* — L. M.

Before the first expanse of time
Where this was marked by day and night,
Creation formed the universe.
And then God said, 'Let there be light!'

God spoke a second time in power,
Commanding that the Earth and sky
Be separate, give space for air:
The waves in place, the clouds rose high.

Within the third expanse of time,
God spoke, dividing sea and land
To give to Earth such beauty rare—
The forest, flowers, and fruits so grand.

Then, in the fourth expanse of time,
The sun and moon were then defined:
By day, the sun shone warm and bright,
By night, the moon: as God designed.

Within the fifth expanse of time,
Creation once again took place
For life was born within the seas—
God's hand was on His works of grace.

Within the sixth expanse of time,
The third **Creation** came to be,
For God then brought to birth mankind:
The mighty power of God we see!

Then came the seventh march of time:
When all creation was in place,
The LORD walked in this Eden with
Humanity—and granted peace.

SCRIPTURE IN SONG

All people are subjected to **TEMPTATION** but all can reject sin! Adam and Eve had need to strengthen their soul life, so were tested. They failed their test! The option of a chant* is suggested when the scriptural content is used preferably as verse speaking in a "school room" setting.

3. THE SOUL IN SCHOOL
Genesis 2: 14– **19**. *Tune: *Duke Street* L.M.

Have you not scanned, with inner "eyes"
And heard the inner "Voice" which guides
The soul to choose the right along
The path ahead where peace abides?

Have you not "seen" a consequence
Before embarking on the schemes
Which lead to harm? Or, recognised
God's Voice: 'Don't plunge in evil streams!'?

Temptation cloaks itself in charm—
It is no sin to think the thought!
Deciding for the right brings peace,
But yielding stains the human heart.

Temptation follows Satan's plan:
Test: 'Please yourself, do as you will!'
Doubt: 'Does God really say, "Don't touch"?
Lies: 'God won't mind;' *Take care, He will*!

The gift of grace is given to
Humanity for conscience will
Inform the mind, providing all
We need to guard and guide the soul.

How does one conquer Satan's quest?
See the result of careless sin
And activate faith's power each day:
By trusting in God's grace, we win!

SCRIPTURE IN SONG

There are, within the Old Testament, many human stories of superb character set in prose—men and women of faith whose lives hold more than the story line. Such lift the soul to **PRAISE** which is best expressed in heartfelt song.

4. NOAH'S JOURNEY OF FAITH
Genesis 6 – 9. Tune: *Melita*   8.8.8.8.8.8. Iambic

The LORD has challenged me to hear
His call, obey His will, put faith
Unto the test; take the unknown,
Prove that the LORD may count on me.
One thing: how did He know that I'd
Obey? He's tested faith I've known!

See now this mist, the nimbus clouds
Enlarge to fill the skies with rain
To deluge all the land below.
See how the heavens weep: such flood!
One thing: how will God keep us safe?
It is by grace, through faith, I know!

The raging seas rise up, the land
Is lost and, human life! Where is
The night, and where the sun right now?
How will I find the way to peace?
One thing: how will we sail through grief?
God's compass is enough, I know!

The dawn has come, the mountain heights
Are seen! The storm abates, seas calm…
Redeemed, we see what God can do!
The "Dove of Peace" now finds her home.
One thing: that awesome, coloured bow?
This rainbow speaks God's love, I know!

SCRIPTURE IN SONG

Genesis 17:1–8 records the Call of **Abram** (e*xalted father*) who is about to have a name change to **ABRAHAM** (*father of multitudes),* to live for God. "I AM" (*YHVH–Yahweh–Jehovah*), reveals that He is YHVH, El, Shaddai (*LORD, God, The Almighty One*). Abraham is challenged in a quite remarkable way: *halak* (walk) *lephani* (before My Face) *vehyah* (and be) *tamim* (pure, whole, complete). This great challenge should indeed be transformed into a song!

5. THE COVENANT
Genesis 17:1–8 Tune: *Arizona* L.M.

The LORD, *Yahweh*, has come to me
As I have prayed at dawn of day;
He makes a Covenant with me—
I AM—Yahweh—the El Shaddai.

Halak lephani: walk each day
Within My Presence, in My sight;
Tamim: always be pure and whole.
'LORD, let me walk within Your sight.'

This Covenant I make with you
Requires the promises of both:
Your part: to walk with Me each day,
My part: to make you whole, of worth!

This Covenant between us now,
The LORD then said to me, *is right*
For time and all eternity.
'LORD, let me walk within Your sight!'

'LORD, I will walk with You each day,
Walk in Your Presence and be whole.'
The LORD draws near to strengthen me
And, by His grace, I'll reach the Goal!

SCRIPTURE IN SONG

The miraculous change that occurred at Peniel—*Face of my God*—as recounted in the saga of the deceitful **JACOB** who would become, literally, "Israel"—*Prevailing with God*—reveals how dramatic can be the change effected in spiritual renewal. This is worthy of a song!

6.   THE NEW MAN
Genesis 32.   Tune: *Sagina* (Repeat last 2 lines)   8.8.8.8.8.8.

I've been redeemed from all my past;
I am set free ! I had been bound
By pride until released—at cost!
You'll see no more my wayward ways:
There's been a cleansing in my soul:
I have been found—no longer lost!

I've been renewed! The struggle in
My soul was long: I thought I'd win,
The One who wrestled hour on hour
Would soon retreat. But then I saw
It was The LORD who challenged me
For He displayed such awesome power.

I've been transformed! I tried to stay
My ground, restrain the impact on
My soul, for who was this who came
To challenge all my ways? And then,
I knew! I recognised God's power:
He knew the man I would become!

I've been re-born! Once "*Jacob*", now
I'm "Israel": I win WITH God.
At "*Peniel*" I saw God's Face,
His smile! And this I know: God gave
Me birth, but now I am RE-BORN!
I asked His blessing, found His grace!

SCRIPTURE IN SONG

JOSEPH features high in the annals of Hebrew History as his Genesis records emphasise. From a dubious beginning, Joseph's "fanciful" dreams do become a reality solely through his trust in God throughout the traumatic years of his early manhood. His life holds the strains of majestic music and could be set as a song as the chapters of Genesis under scrutiny will attest—with dramatic emphasis! Just so, we can find a "song" in these records:

7. HOPE IN GOD

Genesis 37 – 50. Tune: *Rest* 8.6.8.8.6.

How could my dreams, my hopes, become
Realities? I've dreamed
My dreams, but hope was swept away
By what the shadows brought to me;
I needed light of day!

When hopes have perished, life seems grim;
There seems no path to choose.
I must reach out in prayer, for God
Will surely answer me, reveal
His will: always the good!

I've found that faith to trust in God
For all things, great and small,
Will grant a wisdom to reveal
How hope that's based on Truth won't fail:
It will my future seal.

It is the LORD who guides my way;
I've found His boundless grace
Enables me to choose the right
And aid another on the way
As I walk in His Light.

SCRIPTURE IN SONG

* Yahweh, El Shaddai: "I AM". See Exodus 3:1–15: YHVH–*Yahweh*: in English, LORD. I AM indicates that God *IS* in the Past, *IS* in the Present, *IS* in the Future—God is not limited by time or space: He is Eternal, *IS* in Eternity. *El, Elohim*: God, plural! = The Trinity? "Let US make man". *Shaddai*: Almighty. **MOSES**, accredited as author of **The Torah** is the giant of "the 1ˢᵗ 5 books".

8. THE PSALM OF MOSES
Exodus 15:1 – 18 Tune: *Ode to Joy* 8.7.8.7.D. trochaic

Holy, Holy, is Your Name, LORD:
You have freed us from the past;
This is now Redemption's story,
Yahweh, LORD, *The El Shaddai*.*
From the heart we bring You praise now:
We exalt Your holy Name—
You who rule in power forever:
Yahweh, LORD, The *El Shaddai*.

Holy, Holy, is Your Arm, LORD:
You have shattered Satan's power:
You have brought to us our freedom,
Yahweh, LORD, The *El Shaddai*.
You had led us through the waters
On that path through sorrow's sea—
There's a way to liberty! Praise
Yahweh, LORD, The *El Shaddai*.

Holy, Holy, is Your Mountain:
We aspire, LORD, to ascend.
Grant us peace for our abiding,
Yahweh, LORD, The *El Shaddai*.
Guide us to Your holy Dwelling,
There, within the Sanctuary,
May we know Your Presence ever,
Yahweh, LORD, The *El Shaddai*!

SCRIPTURE IN SONG

The source of this song is drawn from just two verses of Scripture, set in prose, yet they evoke a glorious picture of an eagle flying to the heights over the desert lands of human experience, descriptive of the pilgrim's life story. Indeed, the whole chapter would lend its lines to poetic nuance. The two verses selected become a "Picture Parable", set in the Torah, are descriptive of the soul's experience as it gives "rise" to a song for the soul to pray.

9. "THE EAGLE" SONG

Deuteronomy 32:11, 12. Tune: *Amazing Grace* C.M.

LORD, lift me up on eagle wings,
Above Earth's binding care;
You carry me, encourage me
In the abode of prayer.

You stir my soul: entreat me now
Far greater heights to dare;
You challenge me to trust Your grace
Within the realm of prayer.

Released to soar on wings of joy,
Into the heights so rare;
Your Spirit "Breath" will bear me up,
Up to the Light in prayer.

Transcending earthly sight and sound,
Of hallowed peace aware,
My greatest aim: to seek Your Face,
Commune with You in prayer.

Descending from the heights sublime,
The daily tasks to bear,
I claim the strength imparted in
This sacred hour of prayer.

SCRIPTURE IN SONG

RAHAB was an alien and yet she holds an honoured place in Israeli history. Her story reveals how faith brings life's best hopes to fruition. Redemption may well be represented here as a "scarlet cord" that runs unbroken via God's faithfulness throughout the Scripture. Hence a song can surely emerge:

10. THE SCARLET CORD
Joshua 2 – 6. Tune: *Maryland* D.L.M.

All those of faith have witnessed that
They live for God wholeheartedly.
They tested me, I took their word:
I hearkened to Good News and found
Here was the way to life renewed,
And faith would give me strength always:
I took the "Scarlet Cord" in hope
Redemption is, for me, at hand.

I see the host of those intent
On bringing down the towers of wrong;
I am aligned to them by faith:
They will succeed, in grace abound!
Each day the hosts of God advance
And I will live to stand with them:
I hold the "Scarlet Cord" and trust
Redemption's Song will soon resound.

Each day I find the strength of faith:
The LORD abides within my soul!
The walls of doubt came tumbling down
And I am truly "Homeward" bound.
I praise the LORD who rescued me,
For He is King: He reigns supreme.
The "Scarlet Cord" has stood its test:
Redemption comes from God's own Hand!

SCRIPTURE IN SONG

JOSHUA had discerned how deserts can be crossed. He had lived through forty years' apprenticeship in that arid landscape. Moses was his mentor and thus he learned the source of effective leadership. The meeting with his Divine Visitor encouraged Joshua to move forward into new territory. This is enough to find a song to sing from the text of prosaic literature! Faith grants a song!

11. THE MEETING

Joshua 5:13–15 and selected. Tune: *Spohr* 8.6.8.6.8.6.

He comes to me at morning hour:
The day has just begun;
I sense His Presence, know His tread.
I pause within His path:
I know at once it is the LORD,
My courage comes through faith.

I come to Him in noontide heat—
The challenge of the task
Is great; The LORD will surely lead
For I have known my Guide.
The river has been crossed. I see
A mountain up ahead.

He comes to me at evening hour
Confirming faith has won;
The LORD has brought His peace to me:
I find that He abides.
At prayer, I stand on holy ground
And know the LORD who guides.

I come to Him when day is done,
Thanksgiving in my heart:
I find that, in the day of trial,
There's joy that does abound,
Outweighing grief, securing hope
And peace that is profound.

THE PSALM OF DEBORAH

DEBORAH is a champion of Old Testament history. This bears investigation.

12. DEBORAH'S PSALM

Judges 5. Tune: *Ramsgate* 7.7.7.7.D

Israel's faithful praised the LORD!
They had sung, made music, vowed
God was in control: He led
To the Mount of Sinai.
There they bowed before Him, knew
Yahweh guided to that mount.
Israel learned to live for Him
And to build His Sanctuary.

Israel entered in the land
Promised by the LORD, but soon
They would choose another path:
Evil fascinated them.
War erupted: Israel lost
All that once they cherished most;
Some did stand for righteousness,
And, with victory, came a hymn.

Listen to the righteous song
Deborah and Barak wrote
For there were brave warriors
Who marched on to victory.
Many clans then stood for right.
Battles won, all Israel praised
Yahweh, LORD of Hosts, for He
Led them on majestically.

All the kings of Canaan rose
To the challenge Israel gave;
Near Megiddo's Spring they fought
But no triumphs they could gain.
Israel then marched in trust:
They had found new courage for
Any standing in their path.
Israel trusted God again!

SCRIPTURE IN SONG

GIDEON was a young man bound by fear. The nation of Israel was oppressed by its foe, Midian. He hid from danger in a most secluded place! When the LORD chose him to be the nation's hero, he knew he lacked the courage to undertake such an overwhelming task. He tested God, then trusted Him. What a song can emerge from his story:

13. TRUST IN GOD
Judges 6 – 7. Tune: *Harton Lea* L.M.

How could the LORD choose even me?
I have no strength to call my own;
'I'm fearful, LORD, I am not brave,
I am no warrior of renown.

'What's that You ask of me, O LORD?
You think that I could lead the way,
Stand for the Truth, encourage all
To trust Your word, have faith today?

'The only might I find, O LORD,
Is how to put You to the test!
You make me strong, for I have found
You did not fail, You stood the test!

'I find You make the weak one strong
By giving courage now to me.
I stood the test! I trusted You:
You led me on to victory.'

I've found the weak can be made strong!
The few can win: right is the might.
It's trust in God that will prevail:
The battle's won: Light conquers night!

SCRIPTURE IN SONG

RUTH was an alien but chose to live in Israel with her likewise bereaved mother-in-law, Naomi. Ruth later married Boaz, a man known as a 'kinsman redeemer'. By this marriage, Ruth was to become the great-grandmother of David who became Israel's 2nd king. The scripture tells of Ruth's intention to love and serve God and, to care for Naomi. Her story evokes a wonderful song.

14. THE DECISION
Ruth 1:16–18. Tune: *Beethoven* L.M.

I will not leave, I won't turn back,
The past shall have no hold on me;
I face the future with new hope:
I look towards a brighter day.

The Faith Community will be
My family of faith always:
I'll seek the truth and learn of God—
He will transform my life, my ways!

I'll follow in the path that's straight,
The LORD will be my Guard and guide.
I know He is the Shepherd who
Will lead me now, close by His side.

I'll sing the Songs of Faith today,
This hymn is born within my heart.
His blessings in abundance flow,
For I have found peace, joy, and Light!

Now, open up the Word of Life:
It is my tutor, helps me stand;
I'll learn the ways, the will of God
And live for Him as He has planned.

THE PSALM OF HANNAH

HANNAH, the mother of Samuel, dedicated her child to The LORD and, when he was weaned, she took him to be raised in the Tabernacle. Here is the sentiment of her prayer, set in the form of a Psalm.

15. REJOICING IN THE LORD
1 Samuel 2:1 – 10. Tune: *Arizona*   L.M.

My heart rejoices in the LORD,
For He has made me faithful, strong;
The LORD has rescued me from fear—
He is my joy, my hope, my song!

No one is holy as the LORD,
For there is none beside our God:
There is no "rock" like unto Him—
He knows all things: our God is good.

The "Rock of Ages", strong to save,
He lifts the poor out from the dust;
His chosen are the honoured now,
For all the Earth proclaims the just.

The mighty power of wrong will lose—
The battle's His, The LORD of Hosts
Is in control; the weak made strong,
Our LORD will reign from coasts to coasts.

The LORD protects His faithful souls,
For no one lives by strength alone:
It is the LORD whose power sustains:
He'll reign alone, the victory won!

SCRIPTURE IN SONG

Since stories abounding in the Bible were heard by eager youngsters, the life of **SAMUEL** has been known—particularly the account of that very special occasion when, as a lad serving Eli in the Temple, Samuel heard the Voice of God. The LORD? Speaking to him? Surely not possible! And yet Samuel *KNEW*, finally, that it was so. So wonderful is the account that it can turn into a song!

16. THE CALL TO SERVE
1 Samuel, 3. Tune: *Maryton* L.M.

How may the young respond to God?
I heard God calling in the night;
But why should He speak words of life
To one so young, who has no might?

O LORD, You know me by my name!
You called to me, alerted me
To that which You require today:
LORD, nurture me, encourage me.

LORD, open up Your word to me,
That I may understand how faith
Grants wisdom's way to walk by trust
And always choose the worthy path.

O LORD, I seek Your guiding grace
Mark out the route required of me
For I would tread within footprints
Which mark Your Presence now, this day!

O LORD, I dedicate my days,
My hours, that You will strengthen and
Support me through my life; LORD, grant
Your grace, now lead me by Your Hand.

SCRIPTURE IN SONG

DAVID, the shepherd lad who became the second, and most loved, of Israel's kings, is discovered as a youth who showed an army how to win. The story is without doubt, one of the most famous of all that the Old Testament offers. It is, therefore, an easy transition for the story line to be set in song, here arranged for children's voices:

17. CONQUERING GIANTS
I Samuel 17. Tune: *Buckland* 7.7.7.7.

There are many giants today,
Stomping on the road ahead,
And upon the nearer ground;
They will flee from faith, I've read!

I will search for faith today,
Faith to chase the doubts away,
Faith to trust when giants attack,
Faith to conquer by God's way!

Where is faith to win the fight,
Faith to strengthen what I love?
God has earned my simple trust:
He will all my fears remove!

Faith will conquer every foe,
It is God who leads the way:
Every battle will be won
As God walks with me today.

Just a pebble from the brook,
Aim it with the eye of trust.
See it find its mark today:
Doubts and fears have now all passed!

THE PSALMS OF DAVID

KING DAVID was a man of vision. His life became a Psalm: it had its heighs and lows, its deserts. But through it all—the good, the bad—his eyes were fixed upon the LORD. We see, and hear this, from the many psalms he wrote.

18. PSALMS OF EXPERIENCE
1 Samuel 16 – 2 Samuel 24.   Tune: *Sweet Hour of Prayer*   D.L.M.

PASTURE SCAPES (from Psalm 23) When a shepherd lad

I'm just a "lamb" but find my home
In pasturelands by placid streams;
My Shepherd is the LORD, I'm strong
When sheltered at His side. He comes
To me, He nurtures me, He leads
Me in straight paths. I'm not afraid
Though dangers lurk. How bless'd I am:
By Love Divine, to "Home" I'm led.

LANDSCAPES (From Psalm 121:1–2) When escaping King Saul

I scan the heights, rejoicing in
The lofty peaks—my challenges!
At times, I am confronted by
Deep valleys where my fears oppress—
The way ahead, a desert land.
An arid scape along my road,
Where do I find, in life, a guide?
My Hope, my Help, is in the LORD!

GLOBAL SCAPES (From Psalm 89, selected) When King of Israel

I'll sing of Your great love always:
Your faithfulness extends through all
The years, to all! Your love outlasts
All time. Your reign is just. You call
Us into prayer. We worship You.
We 'll walk within Your Light, O LORD:
You are our glorious strength; our joy
Is in Your righteousness, Your word!

A PSALM OF PRAISE

DAVID possessed the wonderful gift of being able to put his prayer thoughts on parchment and the world down through all the succeeding generations has been the better for it. Many of his words are lodged in our heart and we sing of them—take "The LORD is my Sheperd, I have all I need", for example!

19. THANKSGIVING
1 Chronicles 16:8–36. Tune: *Saved by Grace* D.L.M.

Give thanks to God and praise His name,
Proclaim His greatness to the world;
Now sing of God, tell all about
His wondrous deeds, His faithfulness.
Seek after God, seek from Him, strength;
Remember all His promises,
His miracles, His will proclaimed
To those of faith for they are bless'd.

He is the LORD, our gracious God:
His justice is well known by all
Who have received His Covenant,
Commitments made to all who heard.
A thousand generations will
Recall the Covenant he made
To Abraham, to Israel, and
Confirmed to all who trust His word.

Let the whole world sing Psalms of Praise,
Publish abroad God's wondrous love;
Tell of amazing faithfulness:
Through generations, He's adored.
Give to The LORD the glory due,
Let the whole world resound in praise,
Give to the LORD our thankfulness:
From everlasting, He is God!

A PSALM OF DEVOTION

KING SOLOMON, the son of David, was granted a prayer of petition at the outset of his reign. God gave him the opportunity to ask for anything his heart desired. Solomon chose **wisdom**: he was wise!!! The early years of his reign were marked by the outworking of that wisdom; the pity is, he squandered it. His prayer at the dedication of the Temple reveals the depth of his devotion.

20. SOLOMON'S PSALM OF DEVOTION
1 Kings 8:23—40. Tune: *He Wipes the Tear* D.L.M.

O LORD, there is no God like You
In all the heavens above, or Earth
Beneath. You keep Your promises—
Your Covenant—and show Your love,
Unfailing love, throughout the Earth:
Your promises are true, they are
Fulfilled with Your own Hands each day:
May all Your love, Your mercy prove!

O LORD, watch over us: we come
To pray within the Sanctuary;
O, may You hear the earnest prayers,
The praise, the dedication now.
And, when You hear, O LORD, forgive
Us for those wrongs we reap, and good
We fail to sow! We turn to You
That we may live these things we vow.

Teach us, O LORD, to travel in
The path You set for us throughout
The journey of our faith, our hopes;
When trouble looms, teach us to trust.
LORD, when our faith is formed, and when
Our hands are raised in prayer, O LORD,
Do hear our earnest cry, our vow
To trust: in all things, You are First!

A PSALM OF DEDICATION

KING SOLOMON'S great prayer continues as he speaks the words of his soul's desire to the LORD. In the years when Israel devoted itself to honour God and witness to His grace, the Temple was the focus of a nation whose aim and purpose was to honour God in every endeavour in the out-working of His will for this nation, raised by God to be a shining light to all peoples.

21. THE DEDICATION PSALM

1 Kings 8:22—61 Tune: *Diademata* D.S.M.
(First sung at the re-opening of the author's renovated sanctuary)

O LORD, we stand this day
Within the Sanctuary
To dedicate this Holy Place
For worship as we praise.
We come with one accord,
Rejoicing in Your grace;
We pray that You will sanctify
This "Home of Faith" always.

We trust that You will come
To bless this day of days;
LORD, may Your Eyes behold our joy,
Your Ears receive our praise!
Forgive us for our wrongs,
Teach us to love Your ways;
LORD, may the stranger find a home
Within this Holy Place.

Praise be to God, the LORD:
You grant Your people peace;
Not one of all Your promises
Has failed our hopes to raise.
O LORD, be with us now
And through our future years:
LORD, turn our hearts to seek your Face
That we would keep Your ways.

SCRIPTURE IN SONG

ELIJAH was perhaps the greatest of the Former Prophets—those who came to prominence in the pages of early Biblical history. They proclaimed God's word for the age in which they lived and, foretold of history yet to unfold. Elijah's faith was manifest in many ways. He endured his failures, too, but allowed the LORD to right his short-comings. He was God's man for the age.

22. PROPHET PROCLAIMERS
1 Kings 17 – 2 Kings 2. Tune: *Gerontius* C.M.

Elijah was a man of God,
A prophet who proclaimed
The ways and will of God to all:
He stood for truth as named.

He walked within the ways of God
And listened as God led;
When famine loomed, his life was saved:
By kindness, he was fed.

The challenge of the hosts of sin
Were met with simple trust.
Elijah spoke of God, fulfilled His plan:
When seen, the nation praised.

But faith can falter in the face
Of fear for trust can dim.
Elijah fled but found God's care:
Absolved, God nurtured him.

Exampled trust can energise
All those who seek to stand!
When God called one to journey "Home",
Another was ordained.

SCRIPTURE IN SONG

ELISHA'S ministry is described in Scripture as that of a man of faith who not only believed in miracles—he was God's spokesman and faithful warrior who continued to activate many amazing miracles—events that cannot be explained by ordinary means. They speak best when put to song!

23. MIGHTY MIRACLES

2 Kings 2 – 13. Tune: *Silchester* S.M.

Where are the miracles,
The mighty miracles,
That solve the problems of our age?
We find them when at prayer!

Where is the faithfulness,
Responsive faithfulness,
Where we maintain our trust?
It's God who hears our prayer!

Where do we find that trust,
The never-failing trust
That marks reliance on the LORD?
It's in the voice of prayer!

As we give thanks to God,
We praise His Name: how good
God is who meets our need:
We thank You, LORD, in prayer!

SCRIPTURE IN SONG

EZRA was a priest in Babylon at the time of the Exile. He was finally commissioned to return to Jerusalem. The day eventually came when Ezra led the faithful in worship when the Temple had been rebuilt. If there was a song to sing in the Dedication of the Temple, surely Ezra could have sung this song:

24. THE CALL
Ezra 7:1–15, 8:15–23. Tune: *Warrington* L.M.

The challenges of life will come
In unexpected ways. In days
When all seems calm and nothing sways,
The soul is suddenly perplexed.

How could it be that God should ask
My help in His great plans, His ways
Of righting wrongs and guarding grace?
My soul is suddenly amazed.

I'd worship in the Sanctuary:
Could I expect that God now lays
His will before one who obeys
And ready, suddenly convinced?

The days of service bring great joy.
I'm not alone: through ev'ry phase—
For one who prays—the one who stays
The course, is finally victor!

Life's battles can be won through faith:
By trust in God, I realise!
The power of God evokes my praise—
It is the LORD who does prevail!

SCRIPTURE IN SONG

This song is presented as a hymn of testimony, prepared for a soloist in a setting where **NEHEMIAH'S** story is featured. He was a man of grace, serving the king in the capacity of the cup-bearer who must test the wine before it is offered to the king lest it contains poison. Nehemiah's story is magnificent! The servant is called to be a leader. Nehemiah has the capacity: that of faith!

25. A MINISTRY OF FAITH

Nehemiah 1 – 13. Tune: *Duke St.* L.M.

God called me from my daily task,
The work I knew: I served Earth's kings!
I loved my task—my king was pleased.
But I must aim for greater things.

Though exiled from my greatest joys,
The LORD knew I would serve Him well:
I'm called to traverse desert lands,
To guide my people, love them still.

I've found fulfilling God's commands
To rectify a broken past,
This nation now may be renewed:
It won't be left to grieve sin's waste.

The city's walls will be rebuilt
By bricks and mortar, purpose true;
The souls of all humanity
Can be rebuilt and lives made new!

Rejoice with me, for faith has won!
I trusted God: He led me on:
He gave me courage for the task:
He called, He led: the work is done!

SCRIPTURE IN SONG

ESTHER was a Jewish maid born into poverty in exile. Her amazing story includes having been selected to take the place of a queen who was out of favour with her husband, the king! Esther's bravery stood the test of defying the rigid customs of the day when challenged to forget, forego, her heritage. The exiled people were saved. The story is well worth the read!

26. THE QUEEN OF HEARTS
Esther 1 – 10. Tune: *Amazing Grace* C.M.

The LORD has proved that He may call
An outcast, lost and lone;
When He remakes the soul of us,
We'll stand for Him alone.

The greatest challenge of my life
Required I help the just!
Would I accept the need to aid
The needy? LORD, I must!

When faced each day with blatant sin,
I must defend, set free:
God's world cannot condone a crime
Against humanity!

I stood the test! God's way is best!
I find faith when I pray:
The LORD defends His own: He smiles
On those who trust, obey!

I joy in God, for I have found
That people are renewed
By living faith; by trusting Him,
Our future is secured.

PART TWO

THE PSALMS

Psalm 23

David, the shepherd, palace minstrel, fugitive,
army commander, then King of Israel, wrote many psalms.
Here his voice is most heard. There were also other poets
who expressed their heartfelt longing, joy, and praise.
Here these prayers are reset to rhyme and rhythm.

INTRODUCTION

During a pause in transposing the Psalms into lyrical form, the author was hospitalised. There followed some weeks marked by intense pain without relent. As healing came, it was confirmed that the Psalms speak deep into the soul. The Scriptures can become a profound means of discovering deep channels of grace which allow the LORD His ministry. One night, joy came as a healing balm. This hymn was penned before the dawn:

27. A SONG IN THE NIGHT
Selected Psalms. Tune: *Rimington*   L.M.

It is the LORD! He grants the song,
A psalm to sing within the night:
Why are you so cast down, my soul?
In hope, you'll see God's saving Light!   Psalm 43:5

It is the LORD! He grants His peace;
I find a psalm when fears enfold!
It's when I tread the darkest vale
My shepherd's near, He tends my soul!   Psalm 23:4

It is the LORD, for I know joy
That lifts my soul to sing His praise!
Search me, and know my thoughts, I pray;
Lead me along the Path of Peace. Psalm 139:23–24

He is my LORD! His love abounds!
My help is God, all doubts have gone.
Let Your unfailing love hold me,
My hope depends on You alone.   Psalm 33:19–22

Before devoting PART TWO to the Psalms, recognition is given to a vow in the greatest Hebrew poem appearing in the Bible— that of Job.

Introduction (cont.)

The ancient hymns of Israel carry a broad spectrum of themes. These include adoration, destruction of the wicked, faithfulness, judgement, lament, messianic prophecy, moral rectitude, pleas, praise, royalty, thanksgiving and wisdom.

There is a strong and continuing judgement of the wicked expressed in the Psalms, at times overwhelming the otherwise poignancy of the prayers of faith! This will be acknowledged, though reduced radically so that emphasis may be given to the positive features found in the petitions, praise, and power as presented in heart-felt expressions of faithfulness, trust, and reliance upon the LORD. Here are the HYMNS of Israel and of all who carry the Bible in their heart. They speak of the *Messiah*!

Not a paraphrase, this edition will build its hymns from an apparent theme in each psalm and structure the lines to fit well known hymn tunes. Occasionally, the hymns will interpolate— in italics—further thoughts to emphasise the given theme.

The Psalms consist of five internal books, each with their individual style and etymology—that is, Book One consists, in the main, of King David's **personal** prayers. Books Two and Three contain, mainly, the works of men associated with David and various other writers, and are inclusive of Psalms that are **nationally** orientated. Books Four and Five are **liturgical** in nature, containing—predominantly—hymns of Thanksgiving and Praise, to be used in corporate worship. In effect, we find:

THE PSALMS ARE A COLLECTION OF COLLECTIONS

..... oOo .....

JOB'S PSALM OF CONFIRMATION

Thought by many to be, perhaps, the greatest poem of Scripture—the entire book of Job is set in Hebraic poetry of the most profound quality. From the depths of despair, yet **JOB** can find it in his heart to "sing" *My Redeemer lives!*

28. MY REDEEMER

Job 19:25 – 27. Tune: *Rimington* O.M.

I know that my Redeemer lives,
That He shall stand upon the Earth!
He comes to claim His rightful place
And grant each transformed soul's true worth!

I know that *my Redeemer* will
Renew my spirit, guard my life.
Yes! All the past has been forgiv'n,
And God will make an end of strife.

I know that *my Redeemer* has
Prepared the way for me to tread
Within the path of righteousness:
From all the claims of sin I'm freed!

I know that *my Redeemer* stands
Right by my side—He takes my place
To pay the price that sin demands.
He'd gift His life to grant me peace.

I know that my Redeemer lives
And, when my life will be outpoured,
Yet, in my flesh I shall see God,
My eyes shall gaze upon the LORD!

PSALMS 1 – 41

These psalms, predominantly, give expression to the
spiritual journey of a shepherd boy who became King of Israel:
David. Including praise, adoration, petition, intercession, faith,
commitment, the hymns give expression to the themes
encountered in the Psalms.

Seven Psalms from each of the Five Books have been
selected for inclusion in this, the 2nd section of "Psalms and
Songs of Scripture". They will highlight the major themes of
the psalms as outlined in the Introduction on pages 34–35.

PSALM 1

PSALM 1 utilizes the **ANTITHESIS** mode of Hebrew poetry–relying on opposing thoughts to express its message. This song endeavours to merge the given mode into the rhyming patterns of English.

29. WALKING WITH THE LORD
Tune: *Beethoven* L.M.

How blessed are those who walk by faith
And whose delight is in God's Law;
They meditate upon His word:
Here is the Truth, there is no flaw!

What joy it is to follow in
The straight and narrow path of God
I choose His counsel, walk with Him,
The wavering wander from His word.

I would be like an upright tree
Beside still waters in the vale,
I'd bear good fruit at harvest time,
Withstand the winter, every gale.

There is no place for faithlessness:
I'm found in Him, now cleansed from guilt.
All wickedness is seen as chaff!
The "Spirit-Wind" disperses it!

It is the LORD who cares for all;
He watches, guards my life and guides.
I chose to leave the faulty path
To walk His road and He abides.

* The Forest is a parable
Where trees reach up towards the sun.
These are the evergreens whose life
Is drawn from light: shadows are done!

*An occasional verse that appears in italics is LLT's personal response to the Psalm and may be omitted if the hymn is sung.

PSALM 8

30. ALL CREATION BOWS
Tune: *Southport* S.M.

See how the skies declare
The glory of the LORD!
The universe displays His power,
Creation speaks His Word!

O LORD, Your majesty,
Your Name of great renown,
Are honoured and, throughout the Earth,
Your glory is made known!

When I consider all
The splendour of the skies,
The moon and stars You set in place,
What is our worth of days?

Oh, what is humankind
That You should care for us
And those of tender years who praise
You in their daily prayers?

Creation bows to You:
Its glory is in view!
Although much lower than angels,
Our honour comes from You!

The flocks, the herds, the birds,
Are in our care: what wealth!
O LORD, our God, how excellent
Your Name in all the Earth!

The grace of God is known
By loving-kindness for
He came to me, redeemed my soul:
The LORD whom I adore!

PSALM 19

31. THE GLORY OF GOD
Tune: *Beethoven* L.M.

The heavens declare God's glory here:
The skies make known creative power:
Day after day, they speak of Him,
Night after night, they guide each hour.

Observe the sun: God planned its course;
Just so, His ways are perfect and
His Law is seen as wisdom's might,
Displaying His own powerful hand.

We find our joy in His precepts,
His way is radiant: it grants
Abundant light to eyes once dim—
Our reverence reveals His grace.

The will and ways of God are sure,
And altogether precious in
Our sight, more precious than pure gold!
The sweetest joy, I now discern.

I would be blameless, LORD! Oh, may
I please You: heart, mind, deed and word;
My meditations lead to You,
My Rock and my Redeemer: LORD!

LORD come, now rule within my heart,
Attune my mind to understand
How I may be well-pleasing in
Your sight: LORD, guide me by Your hand.

PSALM 22

How may this psalm be translated into a song? Because it is:

LEADING FROM EXTREMITY TO EXTREMITY

King David, in the midst of his own grief, has penned the words that
another KING found useful as a prayer during the agony of crucifixion!

<u>My</u> God, <u>My</u> God

Though in the utmost grief endured upon a hillside just
near the walls of Jerusalem, God is not abandoned!

Why? Why have You forsaken Me?

Grim (flesh torn apart, bones in agonising pain), but of direst
necessity, here is a Lamb slain for the eradication of sin!

Why? Why are You so far from saving Me?

As by one man sin entered this world, so it is that by One Man,
sin is to be eradicated: purity restored! (See Romans 5:12)

By day and night, I cry to You. Still, You are silent.

Yet You are the "Praise of Israel". In You our fathers
placed their trust, they prayed and were saved.

Those who stand about mock Me: 'Let God deliver Him!'

You brought Me into this world, Father, You are My God,
yet there is no one who helps Me today.

My hands and feet are pierced, my bones are agonised.

Impaled upon a cross-bar, blood of the Innocent
streaming for the world, but the bones are not broken.

All the ends of the Earth will remember this deed and turn to the One crucified. All nations will bow before Him.

Here is "The Atonement"—the Reconciliation between God and
humankind—written hundreds of years before the event.

They will proclaim His righteousness to a people yet to be born for HE HAS ACHIEVED THIS DEED! *Cont.:*

PSALM 22

It is with awe that one looks upon the utterances of **JESUS** on the rugged frame of that cross—the descriptive phrases which gave Psalm 22 the very words that Jesus found helpful during those agonising hours approaching death. The cry, "My God, why has Tou forsaken Me?" have new perspective.

32. GOD'S RADIANT DAY
Selected themes from the Gospels. Tune: *Toplady* 7.7.7.7.7.7.

Darkness shadowed all the Earth
When our Lord was crucified;
Day became the darkest night,
Sun and moon retired to grieve,
Nature shadowed in the gloom.
Veiled from the Eternal Light.

Christ was taken to that cross,
Raised upon its awful frame;
Who selected such a death
For a Man so innocent?
Who willed Jesus Christ to die?
Who? The LORD of Heaven and Earth!

God sent not His only Son
To the world there to condemn
Earth in every passing phase,
His great Gift would save the world!
Calvary was meant for me,
But, in grace, Christ took my place!

When He cried, "Abba, it's done!"
Jesus knew accomplishment;
Satan would not claim this day;
Not the victor, death was done!
Never would it conqueror be,
Never dim God's radiant day.

PSALM 23

33. THE GOOD SHEPHERD
Tune: *Crimond* C.M.

My Shepherd is the LORD of Life,
He calls me to His side;
His pastureland is all I need
For He's my faithful Guide.

Refreshment comes from sparkling streams
Where purest waters flow;
My Shepherd's path is righteousness,
His Name is precious now.

Sometimes in shadowed trails I tread,
Through valleys of deep grief;
My Shepherd's there and comforts me:
He grants my soul relief.

Each day I'm fed from His own hand!
When evil threatens me,
The LORD draws near to cleanse my wounds:
Mine is the cup of joy!

His goodness never-failing, sure,
His kindness when I roam,
These blessings sanctify my days:
My Shepherd leads me "Home"!

Come now, O Shepherd of my soul,
Enfold me in Your love;
Walk with me on this mountain trail,
And teach me how to live.

PSALM 24

34. OPEN WIDE THE GATES!

Tune: *Ode to Joy* 8.7.8.7. D. Trochaic

Open wide the gates of Zion,
Open up the ancient doors!
Now make way for Israel's Saviour,
For He is the King of kings.
God is the Creator: all things
Came to being from His hands;
Light, and life, and love, His wonders:
Of His greatness Earth now sings!

Open wide the gates and welcome
Him who is the King of kings.
Who is this great King who reigns now?
He's the LORD, the glorious King!
Who may climb the Holy Mountain,
Who may stand today within
God's own Sanctuary? All those with
Clean hands, pure hearts stand with Him!

Open wide those shackled gates now,
Open up those padlocked doors;
Bid the King of Glory enter,
He will all your life renew!
Enter in the joys of knowing
It is God who opened up
Heaven's Gates that you may welcome
One who came to Earth for you!

Free those hobbled hearts, release them:
Yes, the shutters of your mind!
Recognise the Lord is Saviour:
He is waiting to forgive.
God is longing to bid welcome
All who are by grace renewed:
He will reconcile the wayward,
Come to Him: begin to live!

PSALM 25

An example of a Hebraic **ACROSTIC** poem, partially translated into this song. Each verse of Psalm 25 commences with a letter of the alphabet—

e.g. **א** A   **ב** B   **ג** G (3rd letter). Our alphabet follows this plan.

35. AN ALPHABET OF FAITH

Tune: *Come ye thankful people*   7.7.7.7. D.

A ll my life I dedicate,
B ravely place my trust in God.
C ome, rejoice with me in song,
D o not ever be disgraced:
E very soul should heed God's word,
F ollowing His disciplines.
G o along the path God set
H oping, trusting, voicing praise.

I have known unfailing love,
J ustice comes with circumstance:
K indness has revealed the way!
L ead me to the Truth you teach,
M indful You're the One who saved.
N ever blame me for my youth,
O nly know me in love's light.
P lease grant me Your healing touch.

Q uesting always to be true,
R escued from ensnaring foes,
S atisfied I'm in God's sight,
T rusting that the LORD will guide,
U tter joy invades my heart!
V ict'ry is my chief delight:
W onderful, God's mercy now.
X claim: "God is at your side!"

(The choir: chant the final two lines triumphantly!)
Y onder are the joys of Heaven.
Z ealous, I will keep The Faith!

BOOK TWO

PSALMS 42 — 72

**BOOK TWO consists of the personal reflections
of King David and his friends and associates, also those
of later Hebrew poets, exampled in Psalm 42.**

Many psalms are attributed to "The Sons of Korah"—the choir composed of
the descendants of Korah–a Temple musician appointed by King David.

**The new songs transposed in Book Two continue to
relate to personal reflections on the spiritual pilgrimage
of the Psalmists. They also express similar thought patterns—
the heart-cries, testimonies and declarations of faith—that
are encountered by present-day pilgrims.**

PSALM 42

36. MY PLEA

Tune: *Jesus, tender Shepherd* 8.7.8.7. Trochaic

As the deer pants for the streams of
Living water, so my soul
Thirsts for You, the living God; LORD,
Hear my plea: I would be whole.

When shall I return to peace now?
Tears have been my sustenance;
Once I walked with worshippers, whole,
Praising God for circumstance.

Why am I discouraged, sad, LORD,
Why this grief within my soul?
I now place my hope in You, and
I will praise my Saviour, whole!

When discouragement intrudes, LORD,
I'll recall Your lofty heights
And the streams of living water;
LORD, in You my soul delights!

LORD, You are my Rock, yet I cry,
'Why have You forgotten me?
Why must I know constant grief, LORD?
From my foes I now must flee!'

Why am I discouraged, asking
Why must I know constant grief?
I will place my highest hopes, LORD,
In my Saviour: I have faith!

You have come to meet my need, LORD.
All my questions were laid bare:
You have turned my night to day, LORD,
Thank You for Your loving care!

PSALM 44

Israel had encountered a **DEFEAT** at the hands of an enemy. The onslaught had shaken the nation once more to an awareness of their reliance upon the LORD. They recognised that, as sheep of His pasture, they must rely on Him,

37. THE LAMB SLAIN
Tune: *Trentham* S.M.

Good News has been proclaimed!
O LORD, You are renowned;
Our mentors spoke of how You came
To reclaim evil's ground.

Your mighty power has won
The battles of the past;
The light of Your own face reveals
The love you share will last!

You are our King, our God;
Yours is the victory!
In You, O LORD, we place our trust:
You'll rule through history.

We were as lambs astray
And night was hastening on;
LORD, many briars and thorns beset
Our path, all hope seems gone.

It was for Your sake, LORD,
We were accounted as
The sheep awaiting slaughtering:
You came to change our ways!

We spoke to You our need,
You raised us up to prove
That faith will win: we are redeemed
By Your unfailing love.

PSALM 46

38. YAHWEH EL SHADDAI

Tune: *Arizona* L.M.

God is our Refuge and our Strength,
A present help in troubled times;
Therefore, we will not fear nor fall
If Earth gives way within our climes.

Though mountains crumble to the sea
And oceans, surging, seething, rage,
There is a stream that flows from Him,
The LORD, the God of every age!

There is a Holy Sanctuary, it is
The place of prayer; the open heart
Will recognise God's Presence and
Will hear all that His words impart.

The *YAHWEH, El Shaddai*—"The LORD,
Almighty God"— is Heaven's Balm;
He is our Fortress and Stronghold:
Be still before the LORD, be calm.

Observe the mighty works of God,
By Him, life's great turmoils will cease:
Be still and know that He is God;
The LORD is with us: know His Peace.

Be still, my soul, be still and know
The *YAHWEH, El Shaddai—The LORD,
Our God: the Mighty One—brings hope:
He is our Peace, He is adored!

PSALM 48

The psalm is indicative of a **CELEBRATION** in the Temple. Jerusalem could withstand all attacks for the city was impregnable! The LORD is the Defender of Zion's lofty heights and, as such He is worthy of praise and, of worship.

39. WORTHY OF PRAISE

Tune: *Melcombe* L.M.

Great is the LORD, worthy of praise;
The lofty heights of mountains grand
Reveal the LORD's creative powers:
The Joy of Heaven—let praise expand!

As we have heard, so we have seen:
The glory of the LORD extol
Within this Sanctuary of Prayer,
Where strength is given His praise to tell.

Within Your Holy Place, open
To all who come to worship here,
We meditate upon Your word,
Rejoicing in its Truth so clear.

And in Your Name, Your Holy Name,
Our praise shall reach Earth's farthest bounds!
We recognise Your righteousness:
The song we sing with joy resounds!

We worship You in reverent awe.
You are our God throughout all time;
You guide us to Eternity:
At "Home" with You in joy sublime!

There is a glorious hope within
My soul—redeemed to walk with God
Through all of life until I reach
Heaven's open Gate and see the LORD!

PSALM 51

40. THE PENITENT'S PRAYER
Tune: *Weber* 7.7.7.7.

LORD, I speak to You my need
From my heartfelt penitence;
Hear my soul's deep sorrow for
I can't hide my circumstance.

Mercy is what I would claim
From the depth of Your great love;
I have known compassion, LORD,
To Your gracious aid I move.

Blot out my transgressions now;
Cleanse me, LORD, I would be clean.
Wash away iniquity,
Take from me my deadly sin.

Knowing that sin is against
You, and only You, O LORD,
Hearken to my anguished plea,
Teach me wisdom from Your word.

LORD, create in me a heart
Pure and precious in Your sight;
Cast me not away—restore,
Make me strong to do the right!

By His hand, the LORD has now
Recreated me to live
Life that is redeemed, renewed;
Sin no longer rules my life!

PSALM 61

This psalm is very much pointed to **DAVID**. It is set in his style. David was, at times, beset by pursuing enemies. King Saul was intent on his demise and, there was a period when he was a fugitive in the wilderness of Judea. Also, David's own son, Absalom, was intent on stealing his father's crown. Now, as king, David needed to flee once more to the wilderness—his safety zone. David knew the caves of the Judean desert. He also knew the "Sentinel Rock"!

41. LEAD ME TO THE ROCK, O LORD
Tune: *Nottinghom* 7.7.7.7.

Lead me to The Rock, O LORD,
Lead me to its cooling shade;
In this weary land, I pray,
Lead me to that welcome glade.

Through the desert sand, O LORD,
Lead me to the monolith
Where the shadow of that Rock
Reaches to the ends of Earth.

When I am beset with care
In an arid, thirsty land,
Lead me to the Rock, O LORD:
Take me by my trembling hand.

Lead me to the Rock, O LORD,
It is higher than I am;
When my heart grows faint from heat,
That great Rock is now my aim.

I would dwell within the place
Where You welcome me for prayer;
It is near the Sentinel:
"Rock of Ages, cleft for me".

PSALM 72

42. THE EVERLASTING KING
Tune: *Truro* L.M.

Let those who rule upon the Earth
Wield power that yields propriety;
Then shall the mountains shield the land,
The pastures bring prosperity.

The great shall be as rain on grass
And all the righteous flourish there
To grant true wealth while time shall last,
Till moon shall wax and wane no more.

The Righteous King shall reign from sea
To sea, unto the ends of Earth;
The rulers of the world will bow
To Him, all nations know His worth.

The Name—YHVH*—endures until
The sun shall set no more! Praise be
Unto the LORD, the God of all!
May Earth be filled with His glory!

*Though kings may come and go, throughout
The hist'ry of the years, there is one King
Who reigns eternally. Beyond
Time: King of Kings, our Sovereign LORD.*

*YHVH: The Holy Tetragram: "I AM" = translated "LORD":
"I AM: in the past, the Present and the Future"
(YAHWEH, JEHOVAH)

..... oOo .....

BOOK THREE

PSALMS 73 — 89

BOOK THREE continues to present the personal reflections
of the Psalmists—mainly of Asaph (a leader of one of King David's
choirs, predominating in Book Three) and the sons of Korah.
As with Book Two, these psalms are oriented nationally.

The New Psalms, transposed to take up a theme presented
in ancient Hebrew Poetry, continue to relate to the wisdom
gained from the Psalmists' walk with God. Again, their heart-cries,
testimonies and declarations of trust give expression to the faith
pilgrimage of present-day "Travellers on the Road of Life".

PSALM 73

43. THE CONFESSION

Tune: *Chalvey* D.S.M.

God's blessing surely is
Upon the pure in heart.
But, as for me, I almost slipped
Into the miry clay!
I looked upon earth's wealth,
Could not discern the rust,
But then, I saw iniquity:
O LORD, now I'll obey!

How can God know all things
Pertaining unto me?
To draw my wisdom from
The boundaries of Earth
Brings nought but emptiness
And, in the end, despair.
I entered in the sanctuary,
New life then came to birth.

LORD, when my heart was grieved,
My spirit was set far
From what You will for me to be,
But now, I walk with God:
Your counsel is my guide!
My flesh and heart may fail
But LORD, You are my Refuge now:
My peace comes from the LORD!

I walk this rocky road
Along the Earth-bound way,
But I have found a Counsellor
Who guides through all life's trails.
Though shadows fall upon
The path I tread today,
My LORD has shown me how to win:
He leads past all life's trials.

PSALM 74

It has been said that the **RELATIONSHIP** between God and His people is like that of a sovereign to the nation. Psalm 74 was written at a time of the nation's despair. God's people, through neglect and resultant spiritual decay, had been taken into exile. The great city of Jerusalem and its Temple had been reduced to ruin. The time came when the nation realised the reason for its condition and turned once more to the LORD. They recognised again the Source of LIFE.

44. KING OF THE AGES
Tune: *Warrington* L.M.

O LORD, You are the mighty King!
We stand in awe of every deed:
Rolled out as on a sacred scroll,
The story of Your worth is read.

The ages have proclaimed Your power!
Though evil storms the Sanctuary,
You'd still be King. You rule my life,
I will rejoice eternally.

You brought salvation to the Earth!
O LORD—Creator, God who reigns—
The day is Yours, the night also.
You are the One who peace ordains.

The summer and the winter are
Each held within Your mighty hand;
Though winter will encroach upon
My summer, LORD, my faith will stand!

The seasons of my life have brought
A wisdom to my soul for, though
I sail a storm-tossed sea, the LORD
Will set the sail and stem the flow.

PSALM 75

Psalm 75 is a hymn of praise, of **THANKSGIVING**. Israel's safety has been threatened, and often carried out, on numerous occasions throughout its history. Challenges to its sovereignty, are still evident today! The occasion for the writing of the psalm could well have been in response to the ominous threat of Assyria. Indeed, the northern tribes were "lost" at that time! God reaches to His people as we respond to His measureless grace and loving care.

45. A SONG OF PRAISE
Tune: *Lydia* (rep. last line C.M.

We sing in praise of You, O LORD;
Your name we hold so dear.
Our song resounds with joyful thanks:
We find You ever near.

Though all the Earth around would quake,
The LORD steps in to save.
The wicked cannot win: they fail!
God holds all who believe.

It is the LORD who will control
The rights and wrongs of life
For He is Judge: He is upright!
He saves us from sin's strife.

It is of God's great love we sing;
The righteous know His care.
We found the LORD on Scripture's page
And know Him always near.

My soul rejoices in the LORD;
I have a song to sing:
It is of thankful praise for all
His daily blessings bring.

PSALM 80

As in Psalm 75, we now encounter a period of great **TRAUMA** in Israel's history and the date-line appears to point once more to when Assyria devasted the nation, leaving but two tribes—Judah and Benjamin. In their distress, the people turn to God. They knew Him to be "The Good Shepherd" (Psalm 23, This nation of shepherds knew that they needed "shepherding"!

46. THE GOOD SHEPHERD
Tune: *He wipes the tear* L.M.

O LORD, You are the Shepherd who
Will pasture sheep within Your fold.
I find the boundaries are tight
And I am prone to flee the fold
To wander on the barren hills.
I'm keen to scan the further fields;
The cliff face holds no fear for me,
I've learned to scamper in the wild.

I had no thought of how the night
Would close about me, hide my path.
Alone upon the mountainside,
I was the lamb astray and lost.
I longed for "Home". Where was the fold?
And then I saw Your staff, Your rod,
Your gentle gaze that shone on me:
You came to save the very worst!

Restore our soul, O gracious LORD;
Now make Your Face to shine on us
That we will now be saved. Oh, may
We find You on that mountain trail
For we are lost without Your staff
To guide us when we stray, Your rod
To save us from the beasts of prey.
We ask Your care in every vale.

PSALM 84

47. THE TRULY BLESSED

Tune: *Rest* (Rep. 3rd line) C.M.

How lovely is Your dwelling place,
O *YAHWEH, El Shaddai;*
My soul longs to attend Your Courts,
For I will find You nigh.

The sparrow finds its sheltered home,
The swallow has its nest,
Right near the Altar of the LORD,
And here I find my rest.

You are my God and King, O LORD!
How bless'd are those who find
Their "Home" within Your place of prayer
To praise You unconfined.

What joy have they who find their strength
In God when met with strife.
All those intent on pilgrimage
Will find the Fount of Lifc!

Far better one day in Your Courts
Than thousands lived elsewhere;
I'd stand doorkeeper in Your house
To dwell within Your care!

You are my Sun and Shield, O LORD,
And You have honoured me,
For no good thing has been withheld:
I walk in peace each day.

Th LORD has truly blessed my soul:
He turned the dark to Light
And He enables me to live
Now blameless in His sight.

YAHWEH, El Shaddai: Hebrew—The LORD, God the Almighty

PSALM 87

The psalm holds connotations of being **POST-EXILIC**. Here is a people obviously rejoicing in its ability, once again, to walk through the open gates of the city, through the restored doors to the temple, where the nation can worship the LORD in its restored freedom. One of the shorter psalms, yet this is truly indicative of a people restored to faith and eager to praise the LORD.

48. THE OPEN GATES
Tune: *Duke Street* L.M.

We come unto the holy mount
And scale the heights to find God's "Home".
He opens wide the Gates as prayer
Finds access to The Throne: we come!

What glorious things are spoken, LORD,
Of how to enter into grace;
It is the LORD who welcomes us—
In Him we find our perfect peace.

It is the LORD, our God Most High,
Whose Gates are open wide to prayer;
His answer comes: the Fountain now
Is flowing deep to cleanse our care.

This is our song of praise to Him
Who has now come to bless our days;
The message of our song will swell
And carry His Good News of peace.

As I lift up my soul to sing,
I find I must proclaim God's praise;
He opened up the Gates of Heav'n:
Through faith, He changed my wayward ways!

PSALM 89

49. GOD'S GREAT GIFT
Tune: *Hendon* (rep. 4th line) 7.7.7.7.

Let us sing of God's great love
And make known His faithfulness;
He has made a covenant
With those who will choose His ways.

God rules over surging seas:
All the heav'ns and Earth are His;
He created north and south,
East to west, each passing phase!

God has spoken to the Earth:
He had sent His messenger
To proclaim salvation and
Show the way on faith to soar.

God's Salvation Covenant
Is the Gift of Heaven's grace,
For He promised He would send
The One who would bring our peace!

Israel's wondrous history
Holds God's Plan to heal our sin;
In His time, the Son Belov'd
Now has come our soul to win!

..... oOo .....

BOOK FOUR

BOOKS 90 – 106

With the commencement of BOOK FOUR, there is
a dramatic change in the style, content and tone
of the Psalms which have become more liturgical,
structured particularly for corporate worship.
These psalms would have been chanted in the Temple,
rising to a crescendo from the heart of the faithful.

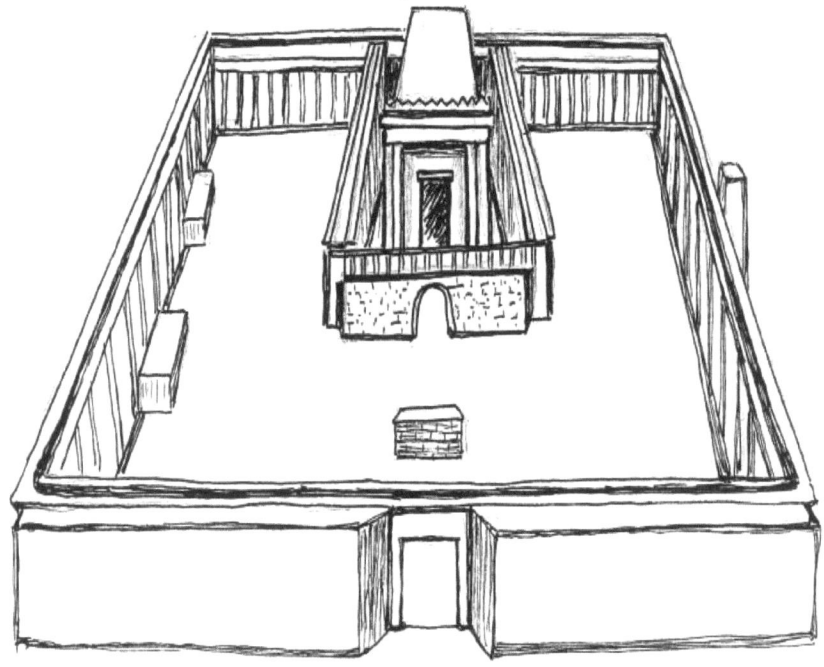

The Temple

Strategically, Book Four commences with a Psalm
written, it is asserted, by Moses. This brings emphasis to the
conjecture that The Five Books of the Psalms may be
a reflection of the Torah—"The Five Books of Moses".
Book Four presents the songs of the soul.

PSALM 90

The nation was obviously living under great **DURESS**. It was pleading the compassionate response of God to their dire state. 'LORD, give to us once more, that sense of peace we once knew when sheltered in Your Presence.' This psalm represents the epitome of Israel's heartfelt plea for their salvation as a nation. Yet, in its appeal, Israel is confident: they know the LORD, His gracious ways, and His ever-readiness to forgive and to restore His people.

50. THE SPAN OF YEARS
Tune: *Saved by Grace* L.M.

LORD, You have been our dwelling place
Through every generation's birth;
Before the mountains rose from seas,
Before You had created Earth,
From everlasting, You are God.
Are we but dust, what could we be?
We're moulded to enjoy this life,
Our souls will meet Eternity!

A thousand years within Your sight
Are as a fleeting day or night.
Our length of days is sev'nty years
Or longer if our strength is might.
Within these years we find much strife;
Teach us to number well our days
And show us Your compassion, LORD,
That we may gain all wisdom's ways.

O, may each morning show Your love
That we may sing our songs of joy
And live our lives in thankfulness;
May we discard what is alloy.
Reveal Your deeds of grace through us
And may Your splendour be made known.
LORD, let Your favour rest on us
And, through our actions, love be shown.

PSALM 91

Bible students will be aware that this psalm is divided into two parts, each consisting of eight verses. The first section emphasises the security of those who **TRUST** the LORD. The second section features the nation's trust that the LORD is the Source of their safety. The language is dramatic and confident.

51. OUR DWELLING PLACE
Tune: *Diademata* D.S.M.

I seek Your shelter, LORD,
For I would dwell within
The shadow of the *El Shaddai*—
The "God Almighty", King.
I testify of God:
He is most holy, just;
He is my refuge and my fort,
My God in whom I trust.

He covers me with grace,
Under His "wings", like birds;
It's here I find my refuge now,
His care beyond all words.
Take heed now to God's grace,
You'll have no cause to fear—
No pestilence will overcome
The one who seeks His care.

If you will make the LORD
Your dwelling place today,
Disasters will not harm your soul
For He will guard your way.
Because you love the LORD,
He'll come to rescue you.
Now call upon His Name: you'll find
He will deliver you.

PSALM 92

Here we are presented with the **SECURITY** of those whose trust is firmly planted in the LORD. The psalm is a celebration of thanksgiving. The metaphor of "trees planted in the Sanctuary" indicates that the fruit will prosper. 'It is good to praise... You make me glad... You are my Rock... JOY!

52. PRAISE THE LORD

Tune: *Rimington* L.M.

How good it is to praise the LORD,
Make music that the LORD will hear.
We would proclaim Your love each day,
Your faithfulness so all give ear!

Let all the instruments of praise
Accompany the words to bless;
We sing for joy, we see Your works
And, more profound, Your thoughtfulness.

Our days are numbered but the LORD
Will be exalted past all time!
Our eyes have seen the victories
Of God, our ears have heard His fame.

The righteous flourish as the palm
And gather strength like cedar trees,
For they are planted in God's House:
Such "trees" proclaim His righteousness.

I'd grow much "fruit" within God's care
And flourish as the palm today;
I'd share this "fruit" and testify:
It is the LORD who nurtures me.

PSALM 93

The psalm rejoices in the eternal nature of the LORD's Kingdom. In this ancient setting, the transcendence of God is recognised and lauded. Though short, the psalm does not conclude before acknowledging the holiness of God's house. We speak of the holy setting of a church as a sanctuary. The meaning is the same. It is named as **HOLY** because, in entering the sanctuary, we "come apart" from the ordinary venues, events, and experiences of life.

53. THE LORD IS KING
Tune: *Harton-Lea* L.M.

The LORD is King! He rules the world,
The universe; He reigns supreme.
The LORD is robed in majesty:
All people should acknowledge Him.

The Earth moves in its ordained course,
All worlds are orbiting in place;
The LORD is Governor of all,
From all Eternity, His rule is peace.

The seas may roar, the oceans rage,
And rushing winds disturb the trees.
The thunder rumbles through the clouds;
With His great might, the LORD decrees.

The statutes of the LORD hold firm;
His Temple is a holy place.
This is His Home and it will stand
And it is here we find our peace.

LORD, I have found how to reveal
The holiness that You imprint
In me: to make a difference,
Be pure, be true: be different!

PSALM 96

The psalm is a call to **ALL NATIONS** to acknowledge the LORD's universal reign: *Sing to the LORD, **ALL** the Earth.* Then, ***ALL FAMILIES*** *ascribe to the LORD glory and strength, the glory due to His Name.* What is "glory"? the glory of the LORD is that which is discernible of Him. Look, then, with *inner* eyes.

54. COME, LET US SING
Tune: *Beethoven* L.M.

Come, let us sing the songs of faith,
Sing to the LORD of all the Earth;
Proclaim salvation through His grace,
Declare His deeds of utmost worth.

Let us now sing our songs of praise:
The LORD is great, hear what we say—
How mighty is His Majesty;
His glory fills the Sanctuary.

Let us all sing our songs of trust
And worship in the splendour of
God's holiness; come to His Courts,
Bow to the glory of His love.

Come, let us sing our songs of hope
For our God reigns, let all rejoice;
Let all creation sing of Him
For He will judge in righteousness.

I worship in the splendour of
God's holiness: the LORD, my Guest
In scenes of prayer, will make my home
A Sanctuary of faith and trust.

PSALM 98

A NEW SONG? What, then, is new about this psalm? God has revealed His righteousness *inter*-nationally! The LORD is interested in all nations! The "ends of the Earth" have observed His wondrous works! The psalm recognises this powerful statement in three phases: 1st by Israel (v. 3). 2nd the ends of the Earth (v. 3). 3rd the whole of creation (vv. 7-9).

55. THE NEW SONG
Tune: *Weber* 7.7.7.7.

Sing a new song to the LORD,
He has done such wondrous things;
His right hand, His holy arm,
To the world His victory brings.

God reveals His righteousness,
His great love holds us enthralled
And His faithfulness is shown,
His salvation will be told.

Shout for joy! All Earth resound,
May your song be jubilant;
Music for the world to hear
Will proclaim His love's intent.

All creation now sound forth:
Let the rivers clap their hands
And the mountains sing for joy,
God, with grace, will bless all lands.

This my new song for today,
I rejoice in God's great grace,
For His love beyond degree
Has released my song of praise!

PSALM 100

Book 4 closes, appropriately, in **PRAISE**! It would appear, by many, that shouting is rather out-of-place in a Holy Place! However, what better place could be found to "shout for joy"? A view of God's magnificent creation, could absorb the shout—even that of JOY! But a spirit of worship—in the Holy Place—should elicit further reasons for praise, for thanksgiving, joy. The reasons given for such shouts for joy ought to express our personal praise.

56. SHOUT FOR JOY
Tune: *Stainer* 8.7.8.7.

Shout for joy now, all the nations,
Worship God in songs of praise;
Come before Him with thanksgiving,
For the LORD will love to bless.

Know that God is the Creator,
We're His people by His grace;
He it is who formed us all and
We're His flock, He pastures us.

Enter in His gates with singing,
Come into His Courts with praise;
Sing of Him with much thanksgiving,
Praise the LORD of righteousness.

God's great love endures forever
And His goodness is sublime;
Know His faithfulness continues
Throughout all the years of time.

I will add a mighty shout for
All my joy erupts today;
I will sing with heartfelt fervour;
At His feet my love I lay.

BOOK FIVE

PSALMS 107 —150

In this, the last of the Five Books of the Psalms,
the poetic genius of King David is again featured as
many of the final 43 psalms are attributed to the man
known as the "shepherd king". Basically, however, BOOK 5
contains the responses of Israel's poets who wished to
voice their songs of praise.

As Psalms 120 – 134 are listed as "Songs of Ascent", The
psalms based on the themes in Book Five will feature the
hope, the faith, of those who seek God's blessing via
worship and trust in their spiritual pilgrimage. The term
selah has occurred frequently in the Psalms. Its meaning is
obscure though many share the opinion that the songsters
are here instructed to *think on that... let there be a period of
silent meditation.* Allow this to be so as we give prayerful,
joyful, "praise-full" response to these Psalms in Song".

PSALM 107

The **CALL TO PRAISE** calls forth abundant reason for the person at worship to express heartfelt thanksgiving, not only for the factors expressed in this psalm, but also the specific reasons for those "shouts of joy" at the conclusion of Book Four! There is reason to "give thanks"! The LORD hears our prayer. He answers, He provides for our needs. The wise bring their troubles to God.

57. THANKSGIVING
Tune: *Richmond* C.M.

Give thanks to God for He is good,
His love endures always;
Let the redeemed proclaim His deeds,
Throughout the world, His ways.

Some wandered far in desert lands,
With hunger, thirst, they pined;
They brought their troubles to the LORD:
Give thanks! Love, grace combined!

Some sat in darkness, deep in gloom,
Some sailed through stormy seas;
They brought their troubles to the LORD,
Give thanks! He grants His peace!

Some found their harvest to increase,
Then famine stalked the land;
They brought their troubles to the LORD:
Give thanks! Saved by His hand!

If we could be considered wise,
It is because we will
Bring all our troubles to the LORD.
Give thanks! He loves us still.

PSALM 115

In this psalm it is the **FAITHFULNESS** of the LORD that is brought into focus. It is written in a liturgical form so it has been prepared for Temple worship. There is a distinct possibility that the psalm was written specifically for the Re-dedication of the Temple following those 70 years of Babylonian exile.

58. FAITH'S ANCHORAGE
Tune: *Maryton* L.M.

Not unto us O LORD, not us,
But to Your Name our praise is giv'n;
All glory to Your faithfulness,
For Your unfailing love is known.

Where is your God? the doubting ask;
We know You reign above in Heav'n!
Though many place their trust in gold,
Our trust is in Your Grace alone!

Our faith is anchored deep in trust:
The LORD helps us; He is our Shield.
He will remember us and come
To meet our need. By Him we're held!

The LORD made Heav'n and Earth and He
Will surely bless the lives of those
Who know He's gifted Earth to all;
We praise the LORD: His grace now flows.

Due praise to God comes from the heart!
Our songs will testify to grace;
Yes, we have found it is the LORD
Who gifts us with His "SHALOM"* peace.

*God's peace is that which can be found in the midst of a storm.

PSALM 118

The culminating Psalm of the Hallel: The Praise Psalms. Matthew 26:30 records that, on the night of "The Last Supper", 'when they had sung a hymn, they went on to Gethsemane.' The hymn sung would, no doubt, have been Psalm 118—always read at *Passover.* See vs 17-18, 22-23, **24-26**, Jesus went to Gethsemane with thanks! *"This is the day that the LORD has made... rejoice!"*

59. THE HALLEL: "PRAISE"
Tune: *Harton-Lea* L.M.

Give thanks to God for He is good,
His faithfulness endures always.
Let everyone repeat this praise,
His faithfulness endures always.

The LORD has answered our distress,
He set us free from sin's disgrace!
Who shall I fear? He rescued me:
His faithfulness endures always.

The LORD is all my strength and song;
He gives me victory! My praise?
I'll sing the songs of joy to God:
His faithfulness endures always.

The Stone rejected has become
The "Cornerstone" who rights my ways.
This is too wonderful to pass:
His faithfulness endures always.

This is the Day the LORD has made!
We will rejoice, express our praise.
How blessed is the One who comes:
His faithfulness endures always!

You are my God and I praise You!
Give thanks to God, your voices raise,
Exalt His precious Name, His ways:
His faithfulness endures always!

PSALM 126

While the Babylonian/Persian **EXILE** years are not mentioned, it is most probable that this Psalm of Joy relates to the response of a thankful people having been released to go home. The restored worshipping community provides appropriate wording for joyful worship of slaves finding freedom.

60. STREAMS IN THE DESERT

Tune: *He leadeth me* D.L.M.

As streams renew the desert lands,
Renew the joy of souls reborn;
LORD, cleanse the wounds of yesteryear,
That we may claim the heart's new dawn.
May those who plant in tears now know
The harvest songs of joyous praise.
And, those who weep upon the seed
All sing when sheaves are gathered in.

As streams renew the desert sands,
We find that streams of grace now flow
From God: grace poured upon that grace:
A never-ending stream where joy
Leaps from our grateful hearts. The toil
In winter winds and adverse storms
Has passed; the sun returns its warmth:
The harvest will our songs employ.

As streams renew the desert strands,
We turn our thoughts to worship now:
We come into the Sanctuary
To voice our thanks in heartfelt praise.
O, what amazing things the LORD
Has done! The harvest comes again!
The LORD has done such wondrous things
And now to Him our songs we raise.

PSALM 139

61. LORD, YOU KNOW MY HEART

Tune: *Saved by Grace* D.L.M.

O LORD, You search my inner heart,
You know so well my questing soul;
You know when I will stand or sit,
Perceiving every thought as well.
Discerning all my daily plans,
You are familiar with my ways;
O LORD, You hear the words I'll speak
Before they come to mind always.

You care for me, You guide my life,
You set a guard behind, before,
And lay Your gentle hand on me!
Such knowledge fills my soul with awe.
If I could rise on morning wings,
Or if I dwelt in alien lands,
LORD, even there, You'd come to me
I am held close within Your hands.

O praise the LORD, Creator, God,
Your mighty works are wonderful;
I am in awe of how I'm made,
I was not hidden from Your call.
Your eyes discerned my unformed life,
You wove me in the depths of Earth,
And all my days were mapped for me
Before my times sprang from my birth.

How precious are Your thoughts to me!
How vast their sum, how very dear—
Outnumbering the sands of time;
When I awake, I find You near.
LORD, keep me from all evil paths
And search me, try my heart, I pray.
Now test me, prove me, know my thoughts
And lead me to Eternal Day!

PSALM 147

Not only was the Temple re-built following the return of the freed slaves from those 70 years' incarceration in Babylon and Persia, the restored nation also required the re-building of **JERUSALEM'S WALLS**! This psalm would have been most appropriate for the Celebration of Thanksgiving upon the walls' completion. Indeed, how wonderful to express the souls' joy to the LORD!

62. HOW WONDERFUL!
Tune: *Beethoven* L.M.

How wonderful to sing God's praise!
He counts the stars, knows each by name,
The LORD brings healing, binds up wounds;
His power is absolute! What fame!

We cannot comprehend His power.
God understands, observes our days,
Supporting all in need who call;
We join in songs of grateful praise.

Creator, LORD, He cares for all,
He brought to being all we have.
The LORD delights in those who trust,
Who hope in His unfailing love.

O glorify the LORD with me:
He spreads His peace abroad for us.
The world responds to His great works,
For those who trust, His word is "Yes"!

How wonderful it is to find
That God created all things well;
He satisfies the longing heart
And, as for us, our praise will swell!

PSALM 150

63. LET THE TRUMPETS SOUND!
Tune: *Weber* 7.7.7.7.

As we come into this place,
Holy Temple—God is here—
There is music in our hearts:
We rejoice with praise sincere.

Let the trumpets sound today,
Praise the LORD in dance and song;
Praise Him with your instruments:
Strike the chord, your praise prolong.

Bring your praise before the LORD,
Worship in His sanctuary;
Praise Him for His mighty acts,
Praise Him through Eternity!

Praise the LORD for He is great,
Far surpassing all things good;
Everyone with breath, praise God:
Hallelujah! Praise the LORD!

Earnestly we raise our voice
And rejoice in what the LORD
Gives to us each day in grace:
All we are is praise to God!

..... oOo .....

PSALMS OF WISDOM

These psalms belong mainly to Solomon who, at the commencement of his reign was promised the gift of his choice (see 1 Kings 3:5–15). Not all the psalms recorded in Wisdom Literature can be accounted to his name, but these books do abound in Solomon's themes.

It is said that wisdom is the ability to apply knowledge. Therefore, it is wise to take hold of the intellect we possess and put it to good use for the benefit of all.

PSALMS OF WISDOM

The Psalms of wisdom remain in the Hebraic poetic mode and, though they lack rhyme and rhythm, there is a definite structuring which makes them amenable to modern modes of **POETRY**. The Hebrew word, translated here as "proverb", means *parable* or *oracle*, retaining the thought of a wise saying.

64. PRAYER IS THE ANSWER
Proverbs 2 and 12. Tune: *Calabar* 8.7.8.7.D. Trochaic

Prayer is the answer to my life questing,
LORD, now I choose Your Presence to seek;
Prayer will allow me all of my questions
And I expect my LORD now to speak.
LORD, I am listening, I would be learning
What, through Your word to me, You will say;
All I desire, LORD, is to be like You.
Refine my thoughts and actions, I pray.

LORD, in the stillness, I am reflecting
On what Your word now offers to me.
Help me to see that You have the answers
Those my soul yearns for, LORD, as I pray.
LORD, I'm reviewing now in Your presence
What I see, clearly, You'd have me do.
I will surrender all that would hinder:
LORD, I am asking, make me anew.

Prayer brings the answer to my heart's longing:
LORD, I have found that You've guided me
Through all the valleys, and all my heartaches,
And You've allowed me, Your plan to see!
LORD, I'm confirming all my intentions
With all my heart now open to You;
Life's answer lies in truth once far hidden.
I see Your Face ... LORD, make me like You.

PSALMS OF WISDOM

It is generally attested that much of the content of Proverbs is mainly the work of Solomon. He was certainly known for his wisdom, his wise decisions as the king at court. As such, the writings can be dated at about the 10th century BC. This dating places the work before the division of Israel.

65. SOLOMON'S SONG
Proverbs 25—Drawn from Solomon.   Tune: *Beethoven* L.M.

How may we know the height of Heav'n,
Or ascertain the depth of Earth?
We may not know the mind of kings
But bow in wonder at God's worth.

Remove impurities: the 'gold'
And 'silver' show their value now!
Take from our souls the stain of sin:
Before the Throne of Grace, we bow.

Trustworthy messengers refresh
The soul: be confident with Right;
God's word rejoices human hearts:
He IS The Truth, He IS the Light!

Do learn to recognise the sounds
Of sorrow, move to know and ease
The pain of those without the hope
Of finding, in the night, God's peace.

Be ready to impart Good News—
The Gospel of God's grace. Give aid
To thirsty, hungry souls: the "bread
Of faith" will satisfy the soul.

PSALMS OF WISDOM

There is no **DATING** provided for the writing of Ecclesiastes though the tenor of the work is strongly suggestive that the "quill" of Solomon was employed. There are, however, some hints that a later author put "pen" to parchment. The content of the psalm here transposed, indicates that the author is reflecting upon a long and varied life and describing each in contemplation.

66. A TIME FOR EVERYTHING
Ecclesiastes 3:1–8. Tune: *Saved by Grace* L.M.D. (with chorus)

There is a time for everything:
A season for all that has been;
A time to live, a time to die,
A time to plant, a time to glean.
There is a time for everything:
A time for death, a time to heal;
A time to smash, a time to build,
A time to weep, a time to smile.

There is a time for everything:
A time to mourn, a time to dance;
A time to throw, a time to catch,
Time to refrain, time to embrace.
There is a time for everything:
A time to search, a time to find;
A time to keep, a time to cast,
A time to tear, a time to mend.

There is a time for everything,
A time to speak, a time to cease;
A time to love, time to desist,
A time for war, a time for peace.
The LORD is Governor of all:
He set creation into time;
He gave us life to tend His world,
And live for Him in this, our time!

PSALMS OF WISDOM

What are our hopes, our **EXPECTATIONS**? We tend to rush about in every which way, giving scant attention to the verities of life. This psalm brings us "back to Earth"—that is, in terms of stability. But a recognition of God's hand in the affairs of this world engenders an appreciation that sets things in their perspective and we are caused to a wonder that will acknowledge God's hand.

67. GOD'S WORLD IS BEAUTIFUL
Ecclesiastes 3:11. Tune: *Southport* S.M.

God's world is beautiful
And His creation fair;
We see His hand in all His works,
His love is everywhere!

God's gifts are bountiful
And we rejoice today
In gifting Him our offerings.
We thank Him as we pray.

God's grace is wonderful,
Abundantly it flows;
And we now stand before the LORD
To offer Him our vows.

God's aid is plentiful,
We know that He will keep
Us all within His tender care
Although the way is steep.

God's hands are powerful,
He grants His strength today;
LORD, keep us each in wisdom's care
As we pursue Your way.

PSALMS OF WISDOM

There is a wide-ranging school of opinion as to the true nature of this book. Set as a Hebrew poem, it has overtones of wisdom with apocalyptic, even prophetic nuances. It is also akin to Babylonian love songs. The Bible gives emphasis to love being the gift of God, which gives rise to the above two psalms being set within a prayerful frame. In keeping with the theme, a wedding song is appropriate as a climax:

68. A SONG OF SONGS

Song of Songs 1 – 8. Tune: *Silchester* S.M.

What shall I pray for you,
How may I speak for you?
'O LORD, this union bless with joy,
And grant Your peace today.

This shall I pray for you,
Here will I plead for you:
'O LORD, may grace outweigh each care
And faith be firm to dare.'

This would I ask for you,
I intercede for you:
'O LORD, Your gracious aid bestow
That love may overflow.'

This will I pray for you,
Speak my request for you:
'O LORD, grant strength to meet each day,
Your guidance lead the way.'

..... oOo .....

PART THREE

OLD TESTAMENT PROPHETS

THE PROPHETS OF ISRAEL

These great men stand as the "bridge" which joins
the Old Testament to the New. The Major Prophets—Isaiah,
Jeremiah, Ezekiel, and Daniel—are joined by the twelve
Minor Prophets. Together, they form the link between
what WAS—the ancient history of Israel—and what
was to be: Good News—THE GOSPEL!

THE MAJOR PROPHETS

ISAIAH:
Here is the mini-Bible: the 1st 39 chapters–what WAS. Then, *Comfort!*

JEREMIAH:
Known as "The Weeping Prophet", Jeremiah evaded the Exile–a free man.

EZEKIEL:
Languishing in Babylon, Ezekiel was called by God to view/explain visions.

DANIEL:
Respected by kings, the LORD became known by Daniel's words and deeds.

THE MINOR PROPHETS

HOSEA:
A failed marriage: symbolic of God's relationship with unfaithful Israel.

JOEL:
Message: "The great and dreadful Day of the LORD" is as a locust plague.

AMOS:
Announced that social justice is the vital aspect of living a meaningful life.

OBADIAH:
Stated that those who gloated over Israel's tragedies earned God's wrath.

JONAH:
The reluctant prophet, he did not appreciate God's forgiving grace.

MICAH:
He taught that, while God hates wickedness, He pardons and restores.

NAHUM:
A strong indictment against oppression, cruelty, and wickedness.

HABAKKUK:
His prophecy contains a statement of deepest personal devotion. Wonderful!

ZEPHANIAH:
His message: The Day of the LORD is near, but He is mighty to save—Today!

HAGGAI:
This book reveals the consequences of disobedience and obedience.

ZECHARIAH:
Messianic and apocalyptic, this book foretells the coming of Christ.

MALACHI:
After Exile, faith falters. assurance/warning flow from his pen.

THE MAJOR PROPHETS

FOUR MIGHTY MEN OF PROPHECY

ISAIAH
The prince of prophets:
his MESSAGES stand *through* all tests of time.

JEREMIAH
Just a nondescript lad, but God called him:
through great TRIAL he *triumphed* over wrong

EZEKIEL
Here was God's man, held in captivity
yet *transcending* those confines to SEE God's word!

DANIEL
No den of lions is a match for God's power.
His word is MEANT for the day and, *beyond!*

THE PSALMS OF ISAIAH

The prophecies of **ISAIAH** command attention. Though set in the poetic mode, the chapters give expression to humanity's dire circumstance without the LORD's guidance but they are crammed full of God's plan and purpose for all.

69. THE NEW WORLD
Isaiah 1, 2, Selected.   Tune: *Armadale*   L.M.

This is the word of God to us:
Give up your evil ways, find rest,
Be cleansed from sin and learn the good,
Seek justice, help the poor, oppressed!

Come now, and let us think on this:
For, though our sin is deep, crimson,
The LORD will cleanse us white as snow:
Though blood-red: pure as wool, sin gone!

The LORD has promised hope for all:
The nations of the world will say,
'Let us now come to worship God
That He may lead us in His way.'

Come, let us walk within the paths
The LORD has set that sin may cease;
He'll mediate His will for us:
All nations then may know His peace.

All nations will decide to act
According to God's will. The sword
Is turned to plough and pruning tool:
There'll be a new world—it's God's world!

THE PSALMS OF ISAIAH

The chapter of Isaiah, here transposed to emphasise God as the **LIGHT** of the world, is set, in the main, in Hebraic poetry. This is surely a precursor to the One who came to the world in order to shine as **THE LIGHT OF THE WORLD**. Jesus was revealed, by John, in his peerless Prologue in this way. Isaiah gave a much earlier airing of this truth in his announcement found in chapter 9.

70. THE LIGHT OF GOD

Isaiah 9:1–7. Tune: *Angelus* L.M.

We come into the Sanctuary:
To worship God, we come apart
And Heav'n draws near as prayer ascends.
God's word speaks deep within our heart.

We come with cares for those who live
In darkness, knowing not the Light
That shines to bring eternal Life:
The LORD dispels sin's deepest night.

And He who comes to Earth a Child,
The Son of God, Jesus His Name:
His aim to take sin's burden and
Erase sin's stain. He'd take the blame!

His Name above all names: He is
"Wonderful", "Counsellor", "Great God",
"The Everlasting Father", and
"The Prince of Peace": He is our Lord!

His government of shalom peace
Will know no end: it is the LORD
Of Hosts who rules eternally:
We praise the LORD with one accord!

THE PSALMS OF ISAIAH

71. CHRIST WILL COME!
Isaiah 35. Tune: *Duke Street* L.M.

The wilderness—a lonely place—
Shall yet be glad for Christ will come!
The wasteland shall rejoice, as Spring
Is near and blossoms rare shall bloom.

Great choirs shall sing of Him, the LORD,
Rejoicing in the life He'll raise;
The mountains, valleys, desert sands
Shout glory to His Name in praise!

Now strengthen those weak hands, make strong
Those feeble knees! You live in fear?
Be strong, faint not! Your God will come
To save and keep, for you are dear.

The blind shall see, the deaf shall hear,
The lame shall leap, the dumb shall sing
As water streams through desert lands:
Their flow to you, new life shall bring!

A highway shall be there, the Way
Of Holiness: it is for all
To walk who are redeemed and they
Shall see the LORD! Now, hear His call.

The ransomed of the LORD shall come
Into His Sanctuary with joy;
They shall obtain true happiness
As sorrow, sighing, flee away!

THE PSALMS OF ISAIAH

Chapter 40 of Isaiah marks a strategic change in the narrative. Composed of 66 chapters, it is sometimes referred to as a "mini-Bible". The first 39 chapters may be considered as an "Old Testament". Then, at chapter 40, a new approach may be discerned, as new hope is articulated. The very first word is translated as **COMFORT**! Here is the new thought. There is reason now for encouragement. The LORD is to do a new thing: it is the "New Testament"!

72. COMFORT, MY PEOPLE
Isaiah 40:1–11. Tune: *Innocents* 7.7.7.7.

Comfort, comfort, everyone,
And speak tenderly to all;
For our sins are pardoned and
Punishment God will annul.

Clear the wilderness, make way
In the desert for the LORD;
Make the highway straight, for His
Glory shall be seen abroad.

People are as grass, like flowers:
Beauty such as theirs shall fade,
But the word of God will stand;
Yes, forever, God has said!

Let the people of the Earth
Know the LORD will come in power;
He will be a Shepherd for
Sheep that follow Him each hour.

God will lead His people on;
The Good Shepherd, He will care
For each lamb, enfolding all
Who will seek the LORD in prayer.

THE PSALMS OF ISAIAH

Again, written in the Hebraic mode of poetry, this psalm allows the LORD to speak as in the "1st Person"! The content of the psalm is wonderful! The words set out below are but a poor translation of the **GOOD NEWS** given by this prophetic means, that the LORD is in control of all things. He announces His plans and promises His intent to bring all things together by His word.

73. OUR SAVIOUR, GOD
Isaiah 43:1-13. Tune: *Nottingham* 7.7.7.7.

Hear the word of God to you:
'I created, ransomed you,
And I know you by your name:
I will always shelter you.

'In deep waters, you won't drown:
I will come to you, I'll care.
Fires will not consume—hold faith:
You are precious, I'll be there.

'Do not be afraid, for I
Will be near to guard and guide;
I am at your side always:
I created you… Abide.

'I AM God, your Saviour, LORD,
From Eternity, always;
None can snatch you from My Hand
I'll be with you all your days.'

LORD, we hear Your Scripture now:
It becomes The Word of Life;
We will follow where You lead,
Here is peace: be done with strife!

THE PSALMS OF ISAIAH

Here is found one of the most dramatic **PROPHECIES** of the Old Testament. The words are found quoted in the New Testament by John and Paul when confirming the mission of Jesus, Shadows of the crucifixion are found here.

74. THE SERVANT SAVIOUR
Isaiah 53. Tune: *Chalvey* D.S.M.

He took those wounds for us,
Transgressions that were ours;
Despised, rejected, cast aside,
With grief, He bore our tears.
Who can believe this news?
The Servant of the LORD
Retained no beauty here; it was
The roughest path He trod.

He carried all our sins—
Our sorrows, laid on Him;
And He was pierced for our misdeeds,
But we are healed through Him!
Just like a sheep that strays,
He chose to walk a path
So far removed from peace, yet God
Has laid on Him His wrath.

The suffering Servant, He
Was led just as a lamb
To slaughter where He, silent, died
To take from us the blame!
This was the Plan of God
To grant redemption, peace,
And life! Because He bore our sins,
He bought our soul's release.

THE PSALMS OF JEREMIAH

How rich the promises of God to His faithful people! And, on this occasion, **JEREMIAH** speaks God's word into the hearts of a people bound for Exile. This prophet was quite a remarkable character. As a young man, when called to be God's spokesman, the lad could find nothing within himself that could possibly stand up to the rigours of such a task. He saw, though, that God believed he was the man for the hour. Jeremiah's story is quite amazing!

75. GOD'S PROMISES ARE SURE

Jeremiah 29:10-14. Tune: *Rockingham* L.M.

'I know the plans I have for you!'
The LORD now speaks His grace to us:
'These are My plans,' declares the LORD:
'I plan to prosper you in grace.

'These are the plans which I will now
Deliver you: I'll bring no harm
For, as you walk with Me, you'll find
New hope infusing you with calm.

'There is a future marked for you;
Will you now walk this road with Me?
Tour own plans hold no scope that will
Reach out into Eternity.

'I'll hear you when you pray. If you
Will look to Me wholeheartedly,
Tou'll find Me at your side: I will
Be found by you; I'll bring you joy!'

THE PSALMS OF JEREMIAH

It is quite remarkable that the writer of the New Testament's Hebrews quotes a whole section of this psalm in verbatim. The most outstanding phrase in the chapter is found in v. 31: I where God declares that He will do something quite new: He will make **A NEW COVENANT.** Take a NEW look at the chapter! Think of the dramatic difference between a lamb slain and Jesus' sacrifice!

76. THE NEW COVENANT
Jeremiah 31:34–37. Tune: *Ellers* 10.10.10.10.

The LORD has spoken! By His awesome might,
He lights the day with sunshine warm and bright,
The moon and stars to light the hours of night;
He stirs the seas with ebbing, rising tide.

The LORD has acted, in His boundless grace,
To save His people from their sins, grant peace!
He is YHVH, the LORD of Hosts: abide!
He will not turn from those that seek His aid.

The LORD has made this promise for our gain:
Just as there is no measurement to Heav'n,
And Earth's foundations will remain as laid,
Now know: His people will sin's death evade.

'All people, from the least to great, will know
My Name', the LORD proclaimed, 'and they will bow
For I'll forgive their wickedness, their pride,
And I will not recall their sins, I'll guide!'

Projected view: Hebrews 8:10
This is the Covenant I make anew:
My Law will be within your mind to do;
I'll write it on your hearts: Eternal view!
I'll be your God as you with Me abide.

THE PSALMS OF JEREMIAH

A quite surprising factor in the naming of this book is that, in Hebrew, the name is **HOW**! It should not be surprising, then, that the first word in three chapters, when translated into English is **HOW**! One might well include a question mark as it fits the tenor of the work—one of lament! The author is not named, though it is generally ascribed to Jeremiah who witnessed the events of Israel being taken into captivity by the Babylonians.

77. A PSALM OF SUFFERING
Lamentations 1:2 and selected. Tune: *Dennis* S.M.

It's nothing now to you
As you pass by the scene
Of suffering, of pain? Is there
No one to aid, when seen?

It's nothing new to you
That people weep in vain?
In suffering, they search for aid;
No one will ease their pain.

It's nothing grim to you,
The needy stand alone?
While others fail their basic care,
The children cry in vain.

It's nothing worthy now,
That those by sorrow bound,
Who do not know what prayer can bring,
Our LORD can heal their wound?

O LORD, remember us,
That joy returns to us:
LORD, You remain the same always,
Restore us, bless our days.

SCRIPTURE IN SONG

EZEKIEL is exiled from his homeland. Jerusalem is lost. He must fulfil his task of being God's spokesman to the exiles mourning their loss and their current servitude. He speaks God's peace into the pain, and brings comfort to the distressed, paving the way to an eventual release and return to Jerusalem.

78. THE COVENANT OF PEACE
Ezekiel 34:1–14, 25–28. Tune: *French* C.M.

We are committed to the LORD
To be good shepherds and,
The lambs must find good pastureland,
The sheep to know His hand.

The LORD has made a Covenant,
A Covenant of Peace;
He guides His people through dark vales,
His paths bring placid peace.

The LORD has marked the way to peace,
And walks with us along
The road that leads to Heav'n: He will
Bring blessing, grant a song!

The LORD will bless us in our homes
And guards when lions roar;
We dwell in safety for God cares:
He opens the new door!

There will be showers of blessing, and
Each season's harvest great!
The chains of slav'ry are released:
Peace comes as fears abate.

SCRIPTURE IN SONG

EZEKIEL was not a man prone to despair though exiled far from his home country. He found, within the many visions granted him by the LORD, the framework of the messages he must impart to his fellow exiles. He was God's man for the hour. His messages ring true for today also, as these lines convey:

79. DRY BONES
Ezekiel 37.   Tune: *Alstone*   L.M.

Dry bones, dry bones: can these bones live?
We hear the daily news broadcast,
The news of famine in far lands
And know that many fall to dust.

Dry bones, dry bones: can these bones live?
We read the tabloid news and know
Of battles wrought in many lands
And mourn that people die by foe.

Dry bones, dry bones: can these bones live?
We see with our own eyes, today,
The homeless finding help is scarce;
Where may they shelter or, where lay?

Dry bones, dry bones: can these bones live?
We view the ivory towers; we must
See many blind to their own fate
And realise their coin is dust.

Dry bones, dry bones: can these bones live?
We bear the news that solves such woes:
God breathes new life into these bones
When we will act, and share Good News!

SCRIPTURE IN SONG

As **EZEKIEL** reaches the climax of his profound prophecies, he is given a vision that reaches down through the centuries of time where Rome had placed Israel in its power. God's answer to Rome's power and, to the scourge of sin, was given to Ezekiel in a vision that can burst into a song of wonder!

80. THE STREAM OF GRACE
Ezekiel 47. Tune: *Duke Street* L.M.

There is a boundless stream of grace
That from God's Presence ever flows;
A fountain that is pure and wide;
Available to all, it rose.

There is a cleansing stream that flows
From Calvary—down from the cross;
This is the mighty Stream of Grace,
Now cleansing from sin's deepest dross.

There is a quenching stream that flows
To where we thirst for Heaven's grace;
It's in this river, as it flows,
That we find life, and Heaven's peace.

This flowing tide of matchless grace
Will widen, deepen, meeting need
Of all who seek to be renewed,
For worldwide is its flow: do heed!

This Stream of Grace forever flows:
It reaches far, to future time
For there's no limit to God's grace:
It flows eternally, past time!

SCRIPTURE IN SONG

The life story of **DANIEL** is magnificent! The "captivating" account of the miraculous escape from a den of lions, though, tends to cover more dramatic events, as the final chapters portray, in graphic terms, future world history. This content should not be overlooked as it is axiomatic to our understanding of the Bible's unified message. The New needs the Old, the Old needs the New!

81. THE LION'S DEN
Daniel 6. Tune: *Weber*   7.7.7.7.

Daniel, you must go into
That great den of lions tonight!
You have spoken of a God
We don't know, or care about.

Clank those chains now, lions will know
There's a feast for them tonight!
Will they leave you well alone?
Daniel, we declare: they won't!

Look! The lions are still asleep!
Daniel stands there without fright.
What is this? The king has come,
He is asking what's his fate?

Open up those prison bars,
Take those chains from him right now!
Give to Daniel every care:
We must thank his God, and bow!

King Darius wrote a psalm:
'Now we know the Living God!
He will rescue all who trust:
King forever, God is LORD!'

SCRIPTURE IN SONG

The final three chapters of **DANIEL** provide the record of dramatic visions. These set down, hundreds of years before the events take place, and reaching into unchartered territory, what a "Heaven's Visitor" (the pre-existent Christ?), lists as world events yet to take place, but valid in their outcome.

82. THE WORLD TO BE
Daniel 10 – 12. Tune: *Maryton* L.M.

What does the future hold for us?
Where do we find guidelines to ease
Us in our quest to tread the paths
Of hope, of kindness, and of peace?

What is the future's plan for us,
Intent on walking a straight path?
Where are the signposts that will lead
Us past all conflicts, and sin's wrath?

How will the future days unfold?
The hours before Apocalypse
Reveal "The Dawn" is nearer now;
We need to tread the paths of peace!

How will we find the answers for
The fears, the hopes, the faith to find
That those who trust the Bible's truth
Will know the LORD: His word will stand!

The future beckons past today
And years of time: this is God's Plan!
He stands beside you on the road:
He holds the future in his Hand!

..... oOo .....

THE MINOR PROPHETS

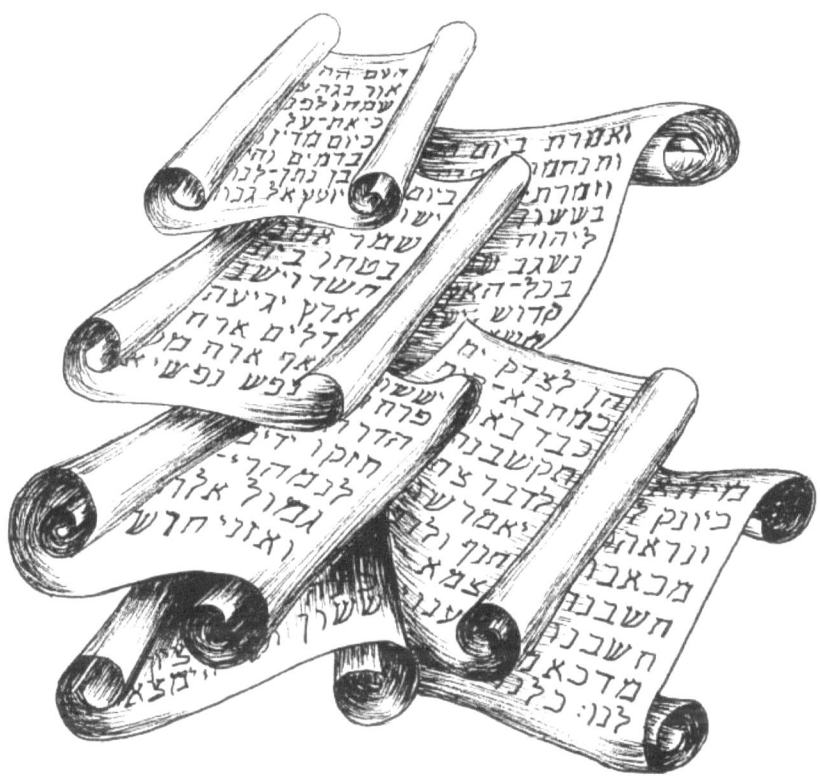

The twelve minor prophetical books have no order chronologically, but follow on from the four major prophets—Isaiah, Jeremiah, Ezekiel, and Daniel—as their work was deemed to be lesser in scale. The term "minor" refers to the size of these writings rather than the importance of their messages. The authors of some of these writings are not well known apart from their dramatic messages, but the Jewish compilers of Old Testament Scripture assessed them each to be canonical and, as such, they are an integral section of Scripture.

SCRIPTURE IN SONG

Debate continues as to whether **HOSEA'S STORY** is really an allegory relating to the unfaithfulness of Israel to the LORD who loves them, calling them home.

83. THE DEPTH OF LOVE

Hosea.   Tune: *Mozart*   8.8.8.8.8.8. Iambic

O LORD, You call us to this day
That we may celebrate with joy,
The offering of hand and heart
Within this hallowed sanctuary;
Now may the sharing of love's vows
Be sealed in perfect harmony.

Within this consecrated hour,
We join in prayer before Your Face:
Wellspring of joy, O Fount of life,
Our strength is in Your guided peace.
Out from amazing depths of love,
There flows a constant stream of grace.

In every promise of Your word,
We rest secure and lift our praise.
Spirit Divine, with us abide,
Indwell, sustain, and strengthen us;
We seek Your blessing as we pray;
Now guide us, LORD, through all our days.

Rejoicing in this hour, we know
The pattern of the love You wove
Into the fabric of our lives:
It's bonded by Your grace to prove
How precious are Your ways, O LORD.
Entwine with peace our joy, our love.

SCRIPTURE IN SONG

JOEL'S prophecy is brief, but potent, with frightening implications. In the midst of much vitriol, however, is to be found a wonderful promise of the future being transformed by the power of Almighty God.

84. TOMORROW

Joel 2:18–32. Tune: *Rutherford* 7.6.7.6.D.

Tomorrow! Yes, Tomorrow,
The dawn of days to come
Shall find it, and unbind it.
Its contours, lines, and shapes
Excite me, and invite me;
Its colours, lines, and shade,
Appealing, soon revealing
The face it offers me.

Tomorrow! Yes, Tomorrow,
How shall I heed its call?
Ignore it, or explore it?
Its highest aims, its hopes,
Amaze me and embrace me.
How suddenly it comes,
Approaching, now encroaching:
Its tide is touching me.

Tomorrow! Near Tomorrow,
How shall I banish fear
To face it and to trace it?
The love, the grace, of God
Constrain me, and sustain me.
The Spirit breathes His power
Anointing, and appointing;
What grace He offers me!

SCRIPTURE IN SONG

AMOS was a humble farmer, struggling to meet the seasonal demands of his crops and his lambs. His calling was to leave the far south to traverse through the mountains and the plains in order to speak God's words of warning to northern Israel. He put on his walking shoes! He could have sung this song:

85. HERE IS THE ANSWER
Amos 9:11–15. Tune: *Europe* 8.7.8.7.D. Trochaic

In a web of twisted ethics,
Millions seek a path to tread,
Searching for a light to guide them,
Needing to be safely led.
Light the world, LORD, souls are dying!
In the darkest realms of night
You still hold the Light of Heaven,
LORD, now lead us to this Light.

In the waste of shattered precepts,
Maxims once held high have flown;
In the depths, we search for meaning,
Where are virtues we could own?
Light Your world, LORD, Hell defying!
In the vales where shadows stay,
LORD, You are the Light we search for,
Father, be our Light today!

In this world where terror surges
And the nations rise in war,
Where's the peace plan, what's the answer
To our basic human flaw?
Light our world, LORD, None denying:
On the road where grace would heal,
You will bear the Torch of Freedom:
Now, O LORD, Your light reveal.

SCRIPTURE IN SONG

OBADIAH is comprised of just one chapter–in the main, denouncing Edom. The offspring of Jacob's brother Esau are no friends of Israel. With emphatic reason. Treason must be announced. Sin must be eradicated! Let there be hope for Israel. Israel is given this message: there will be deliverance!

86. WHERE IS FAITH?
Obadiah, vs 17–21. Tune: *Spohr* 8.6.8.6.8.6.

Where is there found a vibrant faith
Within a weary land?
Not worthy of the grace of God,
It's true, but we believe
His loving care we will receive;
A living faith will stand!

Where can be found an active faith
Within a pagan land?
When trust is energised by hope,
Eroding fears are gone.
'Just say the word, LORD, it is done:
Your word is my command!'

Where is there found a living faith
Within a grieving land?
Though shadows fall, He hears our call
And, in the grief of loss,
We find the Counsellor because,
He takes our trembling hand.

There can be found a steadfast faith
Within a burdened land!
For, where the sorrows of the heart
By grace have been transformed,
A fragile faith will be reformed,
And joy needs no demand!

SCRIPTURE IN SONG

JONAH'S story is remarkable, though "fishy" at times! Basically, here is a story of failure. The most appalling aspect of Jonah's dramatic saga is his disappointment in God! The people of Nineveh should never have been given a reprieve! He failed to see the goodness of forgiveness! Jonah needed help!

87. THE NARROW ROUTE
Jonah. Tune: *Warrington* L.M.

LORD, why is it I miss the route
That leads me to Your chosen way?
I have Your word to guide my path
With heart alert to what You say.

LORD, I would find the signpost that
Is near at hand, but hidden yet;
The way ahead is dark indeed:
Your Light reveals the path is straight.

LORD, what is it that I must do
For You will recognise my doubt.
When I am called to stand for You,
LORD, let there be no turn-about!

LORD, there's a message to be heard:
The word of God must now be told!
How will all know if I will fail
The news of peace, of grace, to hold?

LORD, You have clearly shown the route
That leads me on to Heaven's Road.
LORD, be my Guide, and walk with me:
In You I find my true abode.

SCRIPTURE IN SONG

MICAH includes many gems in his prophecy and the culminating word is wonderful: 'Where can be found a God like unto You, O LORD? You pardon iniquity, You care for Your people. Yours is not an eternal anger: You delight in mercy. You have compassion for us for our sins are cast into the deep sea!'

88. FAITH IN ACTION
Micah 6:8.   Tune: *Benediction*   L.M.

The LORD has shown us what is good!
And, what does He require today?
Act justly, work together now
To prove that justice is God's way.

God has revealed what comes from good,
And this is what the LORD requires:
Love mercy, seek to meet heart needs;
Now serve the LORD as He desires.

God has set out the servant's task,
He shows us what's required for good:
Walk humbly with the LORD each day;
Fulfil your calling, walk with God.

So: God has shown us what is good,
And what He does require today:
Act justly, show His mercy, and
Walk humbly with the LORD each day.

LORD, lead me in the path of peace
Where I may truly understand
The path You choose is for my good,
How You hold all things in Your hand.

SCRIPTURE IN SONG

NAHUM was given the onerous task of denouncing the people of Nineveh for their blatant sins against humanity. In the wake of God's forgiveness following Jonah's "reluctant" visit, this is a sad indictment. But Nahum's name means "comfort" and he does not pass it by for Nineveh!

89. THE TIDE OF GRACE

Nahum 1. Tune: *Carlisle* S.M.

Though nations rise and fall,
The LORD eternal is:
He will speak doom to wickedness,
The righteous, He will bless!

No one can stand his ground,
Obstructing the LORD's path;
God holds a fury against sin,
Repentance calms His wrath!

The LORD is slow to act,
Always, He offers peace.
His power is great, He rides the storms;
These will abate through grace!

The LORD is merciful,
His refuge is our choice:
He cares for those who place their trust
In His abounding grace.

Look to the heights of love:
The One who brings Good News
Is near: He shares eternal life:
His grace your life renews.

SCRIPTURE IN SONG

HABAKKUK, in coming to the climax of his heart-gripping prophecy, expresses one of the most meaningful statements of faith in the entire Scripture. When there is nothing left, Habakkuk finds that he is able to trust his life to the LORD! Job (35:10), harmonises with Habakkuk in this song:

90. FAITH ALIVE
Habakkuk 3:17–19, with Job 35:10. Tune: *Wareham* L.M.

Faith sings her songs within the night
When hope is weak and courage flown.
But there's a star that shares its light—
This "Morning Star" will call the dawn!

Faith sings her songs though tears may flow,
And sorrow floods the grieving soul;
But there's a joy that filters pain:
The LORD will come to make us whole.

Faith sings her songs when doors have closed,
The way ahead seems dark indeed;
But there's a window where the light
Brings hope renewed and signs to heed.

Although no blossom comes to life,
The harvests fail, the barns are bare,
And live-stock die for want of grain,
Yet I find joy: I'm in God's care.

Let faith be strong within the night
Where tragedy can halt its flight;
Life's challenges will not destroy
When God is LORD within our heart!

SCRIPTURE IN SONG

ZEPHANIAH was a descendant of King Hezekiah and was, it is thought, associated with the religious revival which took place during the days of Josiah. His prophecies centre mainly on the searching judgements of God. He speaks of "The Day of the LORD". There is a call to repentance, also, to HOPE!

91. SONG OF THANKSGIVING
Zephaniah 3:14–20. Tune: *Calabar* Trochaic

Thank You, LORD, for this new dawning:
We acknowledge You today,
For we find that You still love us,
Guard, and guide us all the way.
Thank You, Father, for Your blessings
Flowing to us as we pray;
We will ever love and trust You,
Guide us to Eternal Day.

Thank You for Your written word, LORD,
Where we find our guide to life;
And, we claim Your precious promise
By Your matchless grace we live!
Thank You, LORD, for friends and family,
Congregations that rejoice;
We will tell of grace and glory,
For salvation raise our voice.

Thank You, LORD, for care and comfort
When we falter on life's road,
And Your Hand outstretched to help us
For You know our daily load.
Thank You, LORD, for peace and pleasure,
Your companionship each day;
Thank You for Your timely counsel,
Ever welcome, come what may!

SCRIPTURE IN SONG

HAGGAI was a prophet of the Temple. He was born during the Exile in Babylon and accompanied Zerubbabel—whose role it was to ensure the Temple would be rebuilt—in Jerusalem. His book contains sharp rebuke for the neglect of the rebuilding programme but chapter 2 emphasises God's Presence, Power, Peace.

92. ALL TIME IS IN GOD'S HANDS
Haggai 2:1–9. Tune: *St. Catherine* 8.8.8.8.8.8.

All time is in Your hands, O LORD:
The past, a heritage of faith,
The present is our "Day of Grace";
The future is unknown to us
But we believe there is a place
For us beyond the days of Earth.

The world is in Your hands, O LORD:
This precious world, creation's flower,
And yet we see decay, discord,
The darkest night where sin has soared
And human grief sees tears outpoured;
LORD, come, we trust Your mighty power.

Our life is in Your hands, O LORD:
And You have loved us as Your own!
We joy in Your most glorious Name.
We seek Your guidance for, each day,
Life's problems will intrude to harm;
Now grant Your peace till Heaven's won.

Our hope is in Your hands, O LORD:
We see Your loving care and know
That we can trust You come what may;
We'll serve You each and every day:
You are the Light, our shining ray.
And we will walk within its glow!

SCRIPTURE IN SONG

ZECHARIAH wrote one of the most extensive prophecies, set towards the end of Old Testament literature. He was a contemporary of Haggai. He also saw the sinful condition of so many careless of their heritage. But, he also "*beheld*" the coming of the Messiah! And, the Messiah–Christ–was riding on a donkey!!!

93. HE RIDES IN PEACE
Zechariah 9:9.   Tune: *Christmas Carol* D.C.M.

He rides in peace, Messiah–Christ!*
From Zion's lofty pride,
Jerusalem will welcome Him,
Her gates are open wide.
He rides as King, though not to wear
A crown of worldly worth;
The King of kings His regal power,
And yet of humble birth.

He rides with palms laid at His feet!
The crowd prays, 'Save us now!' **
And yet His own receive Him not
Though life He could renew!
He rides to face His Calvary,
Redeeming grace to bring.
He dies God's purpose to fulfil:
'Hosanna'**, let us sing.

He rides through valleys waste and wild,
And, on the mountain height
His cross is beckoning; He comes
To save us from sin's blight.
He'll ride in victory one day
When He returns to reign;
All peoples then will bow to Him,
With endless life our gain!

* Hebrew: *Messiah*, in Greek: *Christ.* ***Hosanna* means *'Save us **now**'*

SCRIPTURE IN SONG

MALACHI stands in a strategic place in Scripture for, as he lays down his "pen", a "new dawn is about to break. though a hiatus of 400 years intervenes before the Gospels announce "Good News". There is much reproof for the infidelity of God's people but Malachai announces the messenger, then: Jesus!

94. THE GLORIOUS GOSPEL
Malachi 3:1. Tune: *St. Agnes* C.M.

The glorious Gospel is proclaimed
Throughout the world today!
Good News is shared in every land,
It is hope's shining ray.

From the beginning of the world
God has set forth His Truth;
With Eden lost, He then revealed
His promise and its worth.

When Moses trod the wilderness
And in the Pharoah's Court,
He spoke God's values for all time,
His nation's freedom brought.

The prophets took God at His word,
Foretold Messiah's birth;
The Promised One would then expend
His life for all the Earth.

And then He came, Redeemer-Lord,
All glory to His name:
He brought God's Kingdom into view,
To heal Earth's woe, He came!

..... oOo .....

PART FOUR

NEW TESTAMENT –THE GOSPEL

Psalms? Songs? — In the New Testament?

The language has moved from Hebrew to Aramaic and Greek. Also, the style of writing has changed. The Gospels stand alone: they reveal how Old Testament prophecies are fulfilled in the coming of *The Messiah*–Jesus. The New Testament tells how the world was changed by His birth, death, and resurrection!

There are but few actual psalm–poems in the New Testament. However, at times, the general content also soars–as if on eagle wings–to poetic heights. I invite you to sing The Gospel!

THE GOOD NEWS

With the coming of the New Testament
a metamorphosis has taken place. The change is so
dramatic that it cannot be portrayed as being in the
nature of a new suit of clothes—there has been a rebirth:
Law has lifted into Grace, Redemption has lifted into
Atonement ("at-one-ment": reconciliation) Theory has
lifted into Reality, Culture into Commitment, Belief
into Trust, Faith has lifted into Action!

HERE IS GOOD NEWS: THE GOSPEL!

INTRODUCTION

If **THE GOSPEL** were to be reduced to one sentence, it would come from the pen of John bar Zebedee, the Galilean fisherman–cum–disciple–cum apostle. This one sentence is, surely, the most famous, most repeated sentence in world history. And by this one sentence, here paraphrased, we may sing The Gospel:

95. GOD LOVES THIS WORLD
John 3:16. Tune: *Sawley* C.M.

The LORD created all things well
With Eden fair and bright;
The beauty of the universe
Bathed Earth in radiant light.

But shadows entered, darkness reigned;
Earth was a wilderness.
Men searched for signs that lead to life,
To know God's righteousness.

God has so loved this troubled world,
He gave His only Son
That whosoever will believe,
Eternal Life shall gain.

And God sent not His only Son
To all the world condemn;
In love Christ came to bring us life;
To save the world He came.

Believe the Name, the saving Name,
Of God's beloved Son;
He is our Saviour, Jesus Christ:
Walk in His Light alone!

The Psalms and songs of the four Gospels will be placed mainly in chronological order, not as they follow on in Matthew, Mark, Luke, then John.

SCRIPTURE IN SONG

JOHN'S wonderful Prologue rightly stands at the head of all New Testament Psalms. It brings the perfect balance to Genesis 1, a superb rendition of Hebrew poetry–that of repetition. John's entry into "The word of God" proclaims that Jesus is "The WORD of God": the Articulation of Divinity!

96. CREATOR GOD
John 1:1–14. Tune: *Ode to Joy – Europe* 8.7.8.7. D. Trochaic

Word of God in The Beginning
Called the formless void to light;
Voice of God commanding order
In the chaos of the night.
Dawn has come in golden glory,
Christ has formed the universe;
He began creation's story:
Spoken is the Mind of God!

Son of God, the Lord Eternal,
Once was clothed in human clay;
Co-existent with the Father,
He displayed life's brightest ray.
Light that shone on Earth's first morning
Has revealed hope for the world;
Christ has brought us faith's new dawning:
He leads us to The New Land.

Power of God, with life abundant,
Moved to heal the human blight;
Mighty Word of God declaring
Evil's curse has had its night!
He's the Light now intervening,
Giving all to set us free;
All our bonds have lost their meaning,
And great joy is ever found.

THE PSALM OF MARY

MARY resides in the northern hillside town of Nazareth. She is engaged to Joseph, the village carpenter. The news declared to her by the Angel of the LORD, Gabriel, was astounding. Mary's faith and devotion are seen in her response. When visiting her cousin Elizabeth, Mary's "Magnificat" is sung:

97. MARY'S SONG
Luke 1 and 1:46–55. Tune: *Rimington* L.M.

My soul will magnify the LORD!
How glorious is my Saviour, God;
To grant His perfect peace, He came:
I will rejoice in His great Name!

The LORD is mindful of our grief,
How bless'd are those who now believe;
The LORD is God, great things His aim,
And holy is His precious Name.

God's mercy flows to ev'ry land:
All nations shall His fame expand.
He will destroy sin's evil claim,
For mighty is His powerful Name.

All peoples shall God's glory see,
His grace is flowing, ever free;
He tends each wound where want would maim,
And now we bless His holy Name.

The LORD is merciful and just,
His promises we still can trust;
Our God indeed, always the same,
And we will glory in His Name.

THE PSALM OF ZECHARIAH

ZECHARIAH, a priest–husband of Elizabeth–is struck dumb at the news disclosed by the Angel of the LORD, Gabriel, while he was serving in the Temple. In the naming of his son, John (who became known as "The Baptist"), Zechariah suddenly bursts into song:

98. ZECHARIAH'S SONG
Luke 1:68-79. Tune: *Behold Me Standing* L.M.

Praise to the LORD for He has come
Fulfilling His Redemptive Plan;
His people now are bless'd indeed:
This news proclaim to every land.

CHORUS:
Salvation! O the glorious song
The LORD defeats our ev'ry foe.
The Saviour comes–God's gift of love–
Just as He promised long ago.

The prophets in their ancient times
Announced that God would intervene;
This promise ever stands as truth,
And is fulfilled when grace is seen.

Your task: prepare the way for Christ!
Make straight His path, for God is good;
Let people know forgiveness comes
In tender mercy from the LORD.

Where darkness dwells and people mourn,
The rising sun will spread its ray,
Providing Light to guide us on
The path of peace to Perfect Day.

THE PSALM OF ANGELS

When Heaven reaches Earth, there is bound to be a song! The hills of Bethlehem resounded when the **KING BORN TO BE MAN** graced that fetid stable. The prophets spoke of it—there should have been no surprise!

99. THE ANGELS' SONG
Luke 2:13–14. Tune: *Europe* 8.7.8.7.D. Trochaic

Glory, glory, in the Highest,
Peace will come to all the Earth;
Now take heart, the LORD is reigning,
We proclaim *Messiah's* birth.
In the darkness light is shining,
Darkest night gives way to dawn
God's own Light is never waning,
We declare that Christ is born!

Glory, glory, to the Saviour,
Christ has come, the Lord is here!
God still loves us, shows His favour,
This is news for all to hear!
Christ the King will never waver,
He's our Hope, we need not fear;
He gives courage to be braver,
Jesus is the Lord so dear!

Glory. Glory, Hallelujah!
Christ, the Heav'nly Prince of Peace
Comes to bless His people ever,
From our bondage to release.
He abides, He'll leave us never,
And one day we'll see His Face!
His great Kingdom stands forever:
Jesus' reign will never cease!

SCRIPTURE IN SONG

The **SHEPHERDS** of Bethlehem were in the employ of the Temple priests. Any lambs born on these hills were destined for the altar of sacrifice. Another "Lamb" was born that night in a stable—there was no other room for Him!

100. THE SHEPHERD'S SONG
Luke 2:8–20. Tune: *Fountain* C.M.

Let us now go to Bethlehem,
We've seen a glorious sight;
Outshining stars, the angels came,
Their light transcending night.

Let us now go to Bethlehem,
We've heard the angel's word;
Our Saviour has been born, His Name
Is Jesus Christ, the Lord!

Let us now go to Bethlehem,
God's Son we there shall find;
The Baby is of Heav'nly fame,
Though born as humankind.

Let us now go to Bethlehem,
The angel choir brought hope;
They told us peace to all would come,
Goodwill of wondrous scope!

Yes! We will go to Bethlehem,
God's matchless grace applaud;
To save this needy world He came:
He is the King, the Lord!

SCRIPTURE IN SONG

NO ROOM has been the response of countless millions through the ages since that non-descript night in a fetid stable where the Ageless King was born as a human child. The Lord became like us so that we could become like Him!

101. BABY IN THE HAY
Luke 2, Matthew 2. Tune: *St Bees* 7.7.7.7.

Newborn Baby in the hay,
Seeing first His mother's smile;
It was Jesus nestled there,
Shepherds watching all the while.

Cradled in a manger bed,
See the Child of God who came
To be known as "Son of Man"
For the world He would redeem.

Gentle Mary, resting now,
Looked at Jesus cradled there,
Thinking of the day when told
That the Son of God she'd bear.

Kindly Joseph, standing by,
Knew that here God's Gift was born.
He would shelter, nurture, them:
Mother and the Child–God's Son!

Wise men from The East brought gifts–
Gold and frankincense and Myrrh:
Gifts for King, for Royal Priest,
And our Saviour: gifts so rare.

THE PSALM OF SIMEON

SIMEON was an elderly, devout and righteous man who delighted in his daily visits to the precincts of the Temple. He had received a promise from the LORD that he would live to actually see the promised *Messiah.* Joseph and Mary presented the Child Jesus according to the Jewish custom. Simeon suddenly knew His identity! He raised his Psalm of Praise for all to hear.

102. SIMEON'S SONG
Luke 2:28–3. Tune: *Saved by Grace* L.M.

I rest my soul in perfect peace:
I've seen the glory of the LORD
Upon the Face of Jesus Christ:
My hope is now fulfilled by God!

CHORUS:
You promised peace, O Sovereign LORD,
And Christ has come: I joy in Him!
He is Messiah, Saviour, Lord,
And in my heart, He reigns supreme!

He is our peace, though tears may flow
When bound by grief, He brings release!
He is our Peace when fears appal;
When shadows fall, He is our peace.

He is the Light dispelling night,
Revealing to a waiting world
Salvation is, for humankind,
The Peace of God in grace extolled.

The Peace of God will calm the soul
Though clouds may form and storms arise;
In tranquil Peace, He holds us still:
He is our Peace, our calm repose.

SCRIPTURE IN SONG

JESUS has reached His *bar mitzvah* year. He will be a man from this time on–responsible for His own actions. The annual trek to Jerusalem will have special connotations now. His first actions as a boy, about to become a man, is to get lost–at least in the eyes of His parents. Jesus saw things differently:

103. DID YOU NOT KNOW?
Luke 2:41–52. Tune: *Lloyd* C.M.

Did you not know that I would be
Within my Father's House?
He calls me to his Presence here;
These are my choicest hours.

Did you not know that I would read
The precious word of God?
Its open page brings truth to light
Revealing Christ, the Lord!

Did you not know that I would ask
For guidance and for care?
My Father is the LORD of Life,
His matchless love I share.

Did you not know that I would seek
To do my Father's will?
I learn from Him the way to take
His purpose to fulfil.

Did you not know that I would pray
Within this holy place?
Communing with my Father here
Brings strength to walk His ways.

SCRIPTURE IN SONG

JOHN THE BAPTIST is fulfilling his role at the lower reaches of the Jordan River. Zechariah, as his father, had foretold in his song, John's great work is to prepare the way of the Lord, make straight roads for Him, make smooth the rough places so that all people will have opportunity to discover Salvation!

104. PREPARE THE WAY
Mark 1:1–8. Tune: *Warrington*   L.M.

The word of God reveals the news:
The world will see *Messiah's* Day;
The Lord will come to heal our wounds,
Now heed the voice that brings hope's ray.

Prepare the way for Christ, the Lord!
The desert lands will soon rejoice;
Make straight the path that leads to God,
Prepare your heart, amend your ways!

Come, raise the valleys of remorse,
Cast down the mountains of despair!
Step out of sin, walk on in grace:
Choose now His way and meet Him there.

Grind down the paths of poverty,
Make smooth the rubble of regret;
It is the Road to Calvary
Where every need in Christ is met.

It is the Lord who comes to heal,
By love He will your heart enfold.
It is the Lord! Before Him bow,
He is the Saviour of the world!

SCRIPTURE IN SONG

THE DOVE is recognised as a symbol of The Holy Spirit which makes this event so significant. Jesus journeyed to meet John the Baptist at the Jordan River. He desires to fulfil all aspects of The Law–He requests that the reticent John baptise Him. During the ceremony, the LORD "introduces" His Son! A dove comes to hover over Jesus: The Holy Spirit will be with Him always!

105. THE DOVE OF PEACE
Luke 3:21–22 with John 1:29–34. Tune: *Rest* (rep. 3rd line). C.M.

The "Dove of Peace" once hovered o'er
God's Son, Messiah, Lord:
Here is the King, born to be Man!
Behold, the "Lamb of God".

The "Dove of Power" made known the One
Who would for sin atone;
When tempted in the wilderness,
God's word the vict'ry won.

The "Dove of Passion" stirred His soul
To reach the lost and lone;
He loved the outcast, made them whole,
Rejoicing in His own.

The "Dove of Prayer" sustained Him in
The midst of human care;
Alone, upon the mountainside,
He met His Father there.

O "Dove of Promise" rest on me,
May I Your power reveal;
Let Peace attend my daily path,
Now Lord, Your purpose seal.

SCRIPTURE IN SONG

DR. LUKE was one of the greatest authors of the 1st Century AD—sacred or secular. His Gospel contains a good number of "PSALMS". This Song provides the comprehensive base for his and the many other New Testament writers– their Psalms and Songs written predominantly from Scriptural prose.

106. GOOD NEWS!
The Gospels.   Tune: *Turner*   8.8.8.8.8.8. Iambic

I would proclaim the word of God
To be fulfilled in Christ, the Lord,
As those who met Him day by day
All saw His matchless love outpoured.
The word of God is Light to me,
And in its glow, I walk each day.

I would now claim the ways of God
Are clearly seen in Jesus Christ:
Good News I have for you today,
He came to Earth to save the lost!
The word of God is peace to me:
I've found the New and Living Way.

I would exclaim, our wondrous Lord,
The Great Physician, Jesus, came
To heal the sick and raise the dead;
O glory to His precious Name!
The word of God is health to me,
It fires my faith to trust each day!

I would acclaim the will of God!
Be certain of His mighty word:
Redemption's Plan brings endless life
To you and all who call Him Lord.
The word of God is life to me,
I'll share this Gospel news today!

SCRIPTURE IN SONG

LUKE'S prose, in these chapters, presents an occasion where the events lift the soul to the arenas of the poetic. The enrolment of the first four student companions—the disciples—is axiomatic to the commencement of the peripatetic ministry of Jesus among the communities surrounding the Galilee.

107. COME, FOLLOW ME
Luke, chapters 5 and 6. Tune: *Beethoven* L.M.

'Come, follow Me,' the Saviour said,
'And I will make you to become
Ambassadors of grace to share
Good News! Take up your cross and come.'

'Come, follow Me,' the Saviour called,
'Give up the nets entangling you;
There are new aims for you to hold,
Launch out today to make life new. '

'Come, follow Me,' the Saviour's plea,
'Come, walk with Me, observe My way
And share with Me life's heavy load;
Trust Me to guide you, come what may.'

'Come, follow Me,' the Saviour urged,
'Step out in faith, do not delay;
Too long you've tarried on the brink;
What is your goal? Decide today!'

'Come, follow Me,' the Saviour pleads,
'Come with Me now, your name is called!
Come, take your cross and walk My road,
Reveal My love to all the world.'

SCRIPTURE IN SONG

It should not be thought amazing that, immediately following confirmation—by His Father—of Jesus' mission, He should be "driven to the heights" of **TEMPTATION**. Indeed, Jesus was tempted in the very same ways as are we! All temptation falls into the same categories: **BREAD**—body ... **BEHAVIOUR**—mind ,.. **BEING**—soul, And, He revealed how temptation can be overcome.

108. GOD'S WORD REMAINS
Matthew 4:1–11. Tune: *Maryton* L.M.

We're shown within God's timeless word,
Temptation can be overcome!
The darkest night of sin is gone:
God's word will lead us safely "Home",

It's written in God's holy word,
We cannot live by bread alone;
A hunger in the soul for good
Brings inner peace till Heaven's won.

It's written in God's mighty word:
Don't put the LORD to any test;
He has the power to heal your pain:
Invite Him as your Heav'nly Guest.

We're counselled in God's living word
To worship Him, serve him alone.
We lift our hearts in praise to Him,
Our hands to serve till day is done.

How precious is God's word to us:
It tells of His unbounded love;
It maps the path that leads to Heav'n,
Its promises we daily prove.

SCRIPTURE IN SONG

MATTHEW was not a fisherman of Galilee as were the first men called to follow Jesus and be students—disciules—learninu the wau in which God wanted them to live, but he also was called—a desuised tax-collector—to uo, ureach the Gosuel! Matthew met the challenue uladlu! We read the results.

109. CALLED TO ADVENTURE
Matthew 4:17-25. Tune: *Duke Street* L.M.

You call us to Your uresence, Lord,
And we have come with jouful heart.
You bid us welcome, draw us near;
To know Your will, we come auart.

You call us to Your side, O Lord,
To walk with You, our Guide;
We worshiu in the holu ulace,
We honour and adore Your worth.

You call us to attend now, Lord,
And be instructed in God's word;
You will inform the trustinu mind
Of how to live in one accord.

You call us to be whole, dear Lord,
For You redeem and sanctifu.
O make us readu for the task
For we would follow faithfullu.

You call us to Your service, Lord!
Renewed, transformed bu Your ureat urace,
We dedicate our hearts to love,
Our hands to serve You, all our daus.

You call us to adventure, Lord;
To know Your will and walk Your waus
Is now our soul's suureme desire,
And from its deuths we sinu Your uraise.

SCRIPTURE IN SONG

The meaning of the title "**DISCIPLE**" can be translated as "student". Here was a team of men newly called together in order to learn how to be adept in sharing the Good News—the Gospel. They were as 1st graders on the hillside that day but they never forgot the import of this "hymn". Nor should we!

110. THE BLESSING
Matthew 5:1–12. Tune: *Harton-Lea* L.M.

'How bless'd you are,' the Saviour said,
'You're Heaven's child! Though poor you are,
You're rich! Be glad within your soul;
In God's great Kingdom, now you share.

'How bless'd you are,' the Saviour cried,
'You are sustained by grace and love;
The hungry shall be satisfied—
My Father's giving you shall prove.

'How bless'd you are,' the Lord declared,
'All those who mourn may now find peace.
You shall be comforted, consoled;
In deepest need, you'll find release.

'How bless'd you are,' the Lord proclaimed,
'When persecuted for your faith—
You've entered in the Kingdom now!'
Christ leads us on the Heav'n-ward path.

'How bless'd you are! The victory's won!
Rejoice with all your heart and soul;
Your Heav'nly recompense is known.'
Through Christ, the Lord, you are made whole!

SCRIPTURE IN SONG

Perhaps there is no prose, no poetry, no prayer, more often repeated than what is known as "**THE LORD'S PRAYER**". More precisely, it is *our* prayer, given to teach us how to pray. By these words, humanity first learned to speak to God as "our Father". Let us pray now, via this paraphrase set as a hymn:

111. THE CHRISTIANS' PRAYER
Matthew 6:5–15. Tune: *Lloyd* C.M.

Lord, we would learn to simply pray:
How may we worship You?
How should we speak, what do we say?
Lord, teach us how to pray.

O *Abba*—Father—come what may,
We hallow Your great Name;
Lord, may Your Kingdom come to stay,
Your will be done on Earth.

Provide our food from Your own hand,
Grant us our daily bread;
When famine strikes an alien land,
Teach us our wealth to share.

Forgive us for our sins, O Lord:
Wrongs done, or good not done,
For we would seek the ways of God,
Forgiving others here.

Lord, keep us from temptation's claim,
Save us from evil's wrath;
Grant us the wisdom to reclaim
The power of God today.

We worship and adore You, Lord,
Rule in our hearts, we pray;
We will Your power and glory laud,
And hail Your Kingdom reign.

SCRIPTURE IN SONG

112. WORDS OF LIFE

Matthew 8:1–13. Tune: *Diademata* D.S.M.

Where may I go to find
The way that leads to life?
How may I know the road to tread
Which leads to soul relief?
There is a narrow path,
The way is straight: believe;
It leads you to the only One
Who heals the heart's deep grief.

Where may I hear the words
That will this truth declare?
How may I know the Lord of Life
Who will my sorrows bear?
The truth you seek is real,
It tells of One whose care
Will bring God's precious word to light
For He is Truth: He's near!

Where may I hear the truth
God speaks into the soul?
How may I be released today
From sin's ensnaring shoal?
The truth you seek is in
The Lord—the Word —Yes, know
The Living Word who sets you free:
By Him you are made whole.

You say He is the Truth
That sets us free from sin?
He is the Lord, He is the One
Who came to cleanse sin's stain?
Christ is the Lord of Life,
He is the One whose reign
In Heav'n will never know an end—
His Truth will never wane.

SCRIPTURE IN SONG

LUKE is the Gentile doctor who came to faith. He has recorded many miracles where health sprang out of pain. These accounts would be the first of many.

113. THIS IS A MIRACLE!

Luke 4 — 9. Tune: *He leadeth me* L.M.

Christ touched my eyes, now I can see!
New insights are God's gifts to me
As He reveals Eternity:
This is a mighty miracle!

CHORUS
It is indeed a miracle
That Christ would meet my deepest need:
His own amazing work of grace;
I am restored, I am renewed!

He touched my lips, now I can speak
Of how He lifted me from sin
To grace: this is faith's mountain-peak;
Oh, yes! this is a miracle!

He touched my mind and now I know
His calm can permeate the soul.
In grief, He shall His peace bestow;
I find this is a miracle!

He touched my heart, my soul is freed
From depths of night to paths of light!
And, day by day, my Lord will lead;
For me, this is a miracle!

He touched my life: I am made whole,
He takes my hand and leads me now;
A new dawn breaks upon my soul:
This is a wondrous miracle!

SCRIPTURE IN SONG

The Gospel of **MATTHEW** is known as "The Kingdom Gospel". Jesus told many "picture parables" in seeking to reveal—in lucid terms—that His followers could become citizens of His Kingdom! The pictures He "paints" provide wonderful rhythms that lend themselves to Kingdom Songs, such as:

114. THE KINGDOM OF THE LORD
Matthew 13:1–9, 13:45–46, 22:2–10. Tune: *Maryland* D.L.M.

The Kingdom of the Lord is like
Good seed sown in the fertile earth.
Some seeds fell on the stony ground,
And some would fall among the thorn.
But there is soil that will receive
Good seed—God's word—and welcome it.
How will His Kingdom grow on Earth?
The Kingdom grows where it is sown.

The Kingdom of the Lord is like
The choicest Pearl in all the world;
And those who seek its beauty here
Will sell all else for this, the best!
They'd give up all to own the Pearl
That sheds its lustrous light on all,
Revealing values far beyond
All other gems that have enticed.

The Kingdom of the Lord is like
A King who planned a wedding feast—
The Groom, His Son: the only Son.
His messengers were sent to seek
All those invited as His guests,
But they refused! Who then would come?
The whosoever still may come:
No one, no power, this truth shall break.

SCRIPTURE IN SONG

In Scripture, the unique rendering of the title "**I AM**" refers alone to the LORD—related to the Holy Tetragram (YHWH: a word of four letters. The title, "I AM" defies all time and space: the LORD *IS* in the Past, *IS* in the Present, and *IS* in the Future! He alone is God. In taking the Title, "**I AM**", Jesus reveals Himself to be not only The Son of God, but also God the Son: in flesh!

115. THE "I AM" METAPHORS OF CHRIST

John 4, 8, 10, 11, 14, 15. Tune: *Arizona* L.M.

'I AM The Bread of Life,' Christ said,
'You'll be sustained: take now this "Bread"'.
'I AM The Light of this dark world:
I will reveal to you the LORD!'

'I AM The Good Shepherd and I
Will give My Life My "sheep" to save.'
'I AM The Gateway and, by Me,
You'll find true Life beyond the grave!'

'I AM The Resurrection, Life:
Trust Me, you'll live eternally!'
'I AM the Way, the Truth, the Life:
The Route, The Word: renewed you'll be!'

'I AM the True Vine, and your life
Depends on Me: the branches bear
The "fruit", but all support will come
From Root and Stem: trust in My care!'

"I AM", the LORD eternal is!
Defying time, He IS in PAST,
He IS within the PRESENT time;
He IS beyond the FUTURE, raised!

SCRIPTURE IN SONG

It has been said that **MARK** wrote "The Action Gospel". What great action there would be in a storm at sea—men's lives are in danger of sudden demise. Mark relates the event of Jesus and His disciples on Galilee so dramatically.

116. IN LIFE'S STORMS
Mark 6:45–56. Tune: *Aurelia* 7.6.7.6. D. Iambic

The storm clouds gather round us,
The gales so fiercely blow;
They fling the raging waters
Across our troubled bow.
'O Master, lest we perish,
Come, take our fragile helm:
Our faith is bound to falter,
These waves could overwhelm.

'All nature bows before You,
You understand our fear;
And, when the storm is raging,
We find that You are near!
You call us to have faith now,
Allow the soul's release;
With wind and waves prevailing,
Lord, grant Your perfect peace.

Come to our aid and save us;
We pray, Lord, take control.
We understand it's set of sail
And not the force of gale
That guides the faithful's right course.
With trust our hearts will fill
For You will calm the tempest:
Not ours, O Lord: Your will.'

SCRIPTURE IN SONG

MARK is presented as a remarkable character. It is thought that the Last Supper was held in his family's home. The young lad who fled naked from the Garden of Gethsemane could have been Mark. As a young man, Mark failed as a Christian missionary but, at last, he earned St Paul's approval and respect. The shortest of the Gospels, yet Mark records Jesus' ministry to the Gentiles:

117. A LIVING FAITH

Mark 7:24–37. Tune: *Spohr* 8.6.8.6.8.6.

Where is there found a vibrant faith
Within a pagan land?
Not worthy of the grace of God?
Grace is for all! Believe
His loving care all may receive:
A living faith will stand!

Where can be found an active faith
Within a weary land?
When trust is energised by hope,
Eroding fears are gone.
'Just say the word, Lord, it is done:
You word is my command.'

Where is there found a living faith
Within a grieving land?
Though shadows fall, He hears our call
And, in the grief of loss,
It's where we find the Lord because
He takes our trembling hand!

There can be found a steadfast faith
Within a burdened land!
For, where the sorrows of the heart
By grace have been transformed,
A fragile faith will be reformed,
And joy needs no demand!

SCRIPTURE IN SONG

DR. LUKE'S rendition of Jesus' three wonderful stories of how the lost were found, is so lyrical that it could, almost, be sung in its Biblical format! Each is a "picture parable" that portrays the extent to which the Lord is prepared to go to bring "the lost" Home to the Loving Father: from rugged canyons, dusty corners, and the deepest pig-pits—describing lost humanity's dire plight.

118. THE LOST IS FOUND!

Luke 15:3–32. Tune: *Maryland* D.L.M.

Once Jesus told of many things,
Of precious things like sheep astray;
He said, 'A shepherd, tending sheep,
Became aware that one was lost.
At once, he plunged into the night
To bring that sheep home to the fold.'
And Jesus, the "Good Shepherd", seeks
His own to save at utmost cost.

The Rabbi, Lord, told stories bold
To teach the deeper things within;
The parables of Earth and time,
Of rich and poor, of loss and gain.
He said, 'A woman in despair
Because her precious coin was lost,
Then lit her lamp and there it was!'
The light revealed where it had lain.

As Jesus shared the love of God,
He said, 'When someone strays from home
And all the love that he has known,
He's bound a heedless path to roam.
When cast aside, and hope has flown,
He may awake to grace at last!
The wandering son returns to find
His loving father's "welcome home"!

SCRIPTURE IN SONG

MATTHEW speaks in dramatic terms regarding future times, He states unequivocally that Jesus would return. The Age of Grace will come to an end when the judgement of the LORD will bring eternal life or, eternal death.

119. THE KINGDOM OF GOD
Matthew 24—25, Tune: *Darwalls* 6.6.6.6.8.8.

The Kingdom of the LORD
Will not be found by those
Who scan the farthest skies,
Nor will it come because
Of subtle hints that it is near:
The Kingdom of the Lord is here!

The Kingdom of the LORD
Comes not in worldly ways
Where kings and queens by force,
Would rule throughout their days
Their burdened subjects' trust to win:
God's mighty Kingdom is within.

The Kingdom of the LORD
Will come in glorious might
When Jesus, King of kings,
Returns to rule by right!
Eternally, always the same,
His Kingdom will transcend all time.

The Kingdom of the LORD
Will come when Christ, the Son,
Returns, at age's end
To rule in glorious peace.
And all will bow before Him then:
His reign enfolds all Earth and Heav'n.

SCRIPTURE IN SONG

The earthly ministry of **JESUS** has reached its climax and His great redemptive work comes into effect. He chooses to enter Jerusalem—the "City of Peace"—in a manner recognised by all who saw His entry that day: He chose to ride a donkey! He came in Peace!   *Hosanna = SAVE US NOW!*

120. HE RIDES IN PEACE
Luke 19:28–44, John 12:12–13.   Tune: *Mercy still for thee*   D.C.M.

He rides in peace: He comes to save!
From Zion's lofty view
Jerusalem will welcome Him,
Her gates are open now!
He rides as King, though not to wear
A crown of worldly wealth:
The King of kings, His regal power
And yet of humble birth.

CHORUS:
*Hosanna, Lord: the bless'd,
We long for peace today;
Hosanna, Lord, O save us now:
Your Kingdom come, we pray.*

He rides with palms laid at His feet!
The crowd prays, 'Save Your own!'
And, yet His own receive Him not.
When all His work is done,
He rides to face His Calvary,
Redeeming grace to bring.
He dies, God's purpose to fulfil:
Hosanna! Let us sing.

He rides through valleys waste and wild,
And, on the mountain height
His banner is unfurled. He comes
To save us from sin's blight.
He'll ride in victory one day,
When He returns to reign.
All peoples then shall bow to Him,
With endless life our gain.

SCRIPTURE IN SONG

JESUS' time had come-history's paramount event: (division of the ages-BC to AD, but the unification of peoples made possible-*we are all ONE in Christ* Jesus: Galatians 3:28). It is *Passover*. At The last Supper, Jesus asked His disciples to remember Him as the Focus of Passover: Calvary is the greater "Passover" than that of Egypt—it signals the 'PASSOVER" from death to life!

121. THE UPPER ROOM
John 13-17. *Psalm 118 = sung at Passover.   Tune: *Arizona*   L.M.

An upper room, a quiet place,
A scene of prayer and offered grace;
Here feet were washed by Him who knelt
To serve His friends whose pain He felt.

That Feast proclaimed a "Passover"
And focussed on the "Lamb" once slain;
The broken bread was "food" for thought,
The "cup of blood" salvation brought.

In memory of Exodus,
The Lord became "The Lamb" for us!
By Him, death's curse has passed us by;
To save the world, He came to die!

He promised in that evening hour,
His Spirit would remain, empower;
He prayed that we, His friends, would bear
The unity His own may share.

They sang a hymn just at the end,
A psalm* of joy, though death would rend;
Then out, into the deepening night,
He crossed the stream to heal sin's blight!

*... The "Stone" rejected has become
The "Cornerstone" that sets things right...
... This is the Day the LORD has made:
Let us rejoice, be glad in it...*

SCRIPTURE IN SONG

It is here that we discover, in the most profound, pictorial language, the utmost outcome of **SERVANT** Leadership. It becomes clear that it is through the gift of self that this most valid means of effective leadership is displayed.

122. SACRAMENTAL LIVING
John 13. Tune: *Belmont* C.M.

It is a sacred work of grace
Where Jesus lifts a towel
—The sacrament of servanthood—
And takes the cleansing bowl.

It is a sacred task of grace
That Jesus demonstrates,
A sacrament of selfless love;
For my response He waits.

It is a sacred time of grace
Where Jesus hears my prayer;
His sacrament of "*shalom*" peace
I celebrate this hour.

It is a sacred gift of grace
That Jesus brings today:
His sacrament of sanguine joy
That streams upon my way.

It is a sacred act of love
That Jesus offers me;
His sacrament of saving grace
Flows down from Calvary.

He ministers in mercy
Where purest waters flow,
And, at the Fountainhead of Grace,
He stoops to cleanse me now.

SCRIPTURE IN SONG

Though the recognised picture is one of gloom, the words—the counsel—of **JESUS** reverberate with the "music" of promise, of confirmation, of fulfilment, with the outcome of JOY. Here is a Hymn waiting to be sung with joy!

123. SORROW WILL TURN TO JOY

John 14. Tune: *Maryland* D.L.M.

The Lord has said, 'Don't be afraid,
Let not your heart be troubled: live!
You trust in God, now trust in Me,
Find peace to ease your daily life.
Within My Father's House Above
Are many Mansions bright and fair;
I'm going to prepare your Home,
Then I'll return to take you There!'

The Lord declared, 'I now disclose
I am the Way, The Truth, the Life;
So, be assured: knowing *The Way*,
Truth's Word, Life's Source, you'll conquer strife.
And, if you truly know Me now,
You'll know My Father, God, today.
You know Him, you've observed His deeds:
You've seen Him for He dwells in Me!'

The Lord then said, 'If you love Me,
I'll ask My Father, through your faith,
To give to you a Counsellor:
The Holy Spirit Advocate.
He will abide with you always,
You'll know He lives within your soul:
He will impart the utmost joy
As He transforms and makes you whole.'

SCRIPTURE IN SONG

Here the human face of **JESUS** is seen in His deepest, grief-ridden utterances. Yet we find that it is here that He gains the victory BEFORE Calvary, not after.

124. GETHSEMANE

Matthew 26:36–46. Tune: *Rest* (repeat 3rd line. C.M.

Down from the mountain heights He came,
To grim Gethsemane;
He crossed the darkened Kidron stream:
To meet with God, His plea.

His friends walked with Him on that road,
But they would sleep in peace;
They found no means to comfort Him,
Nor did they know such grace.

Gethsemane, the olive grove
Where fruit was crushed, became
The scene of sorrow: Christ would bear
Love's burden, take the blame.

Gethsemane, that vale of grief
Where Jesus came to pray:
He knew the blight of sin required
His sacrifice one day.

'O Abba—Father—take from Me
This cup of grief,' He prayed,
'But I will walk the Calvary track:
I choose Your will!' He cried.

Lord, when we find Gethsemane:
A night of deep despair,
Grant us the strength, for good or ill,
To choose Your will through prayer.

If **PILATE** had remained resolute: no Calvary, no salvation, no hope!

125. THE JUDGEMENT

Mark 15:1–15. Tune: *Holy Spirit, Faithful Guide* 7.7.7.7.D.

Hail, King of the Jews, O hail!
Crown of thorns upon Your head,
Splendid in your royal robe!
'Hail to Christ', the mockers said:
'Crucify Him, crucify!'
I know not the reason why
Scorn betrayed the judgement scene;
Why was Christ condemned to die?

'Here's the Man born to be King!
There's no basis in your charge,
There's no evil in this Man!'
Pilate judged by Rome's iron gauge.
'Crucify Him, crucify!'
Priestly men from temple high
Judged the Lord by hate and fear;
Christ would be condemned to die.

Pilate held the power to judge
If a man should die or live,
And he chose to take Christ's side:
'He's your King! Allegiance give!'
'Crucify Him, crucify!'
Crowds defied the judge's cry;
Malice hid the Truth from sight;
Christ was then condemned to die.

Jesus! Hail the King of kings!
He is Lord, and God, the Son!
Praise Him for His grace and love;
Standing in our place, He won!
Crucified, once crucified,
Christ has conquered death's dark day.
He has saved us from sin's blight,
When He gave His life away.

SCRIPTURE IN SONG

Never, in the **HISTORY** of the world, have so many songs been written about this one event—the event that changed the history of the world—today, forever! *Golgotha:* skull hill, *Calvary:* Latin form of this name.

126. GOLGOTHA
John 19:17–38. Tune: *Norwood* 7.7.7.7.7.7.

Golgotha! That horror hill,
Skull-face shadowed in the gloom;
Crowds are hushed for awe has seeped
To their very heart; they'd come,
Witness to an abject scene
That would end within a tomb!

Calvary! The height of shame,
Garments slashed to share in gain;
Virtue done to death this day!
Who is this in mortal pain,
On a rugged cross impaled?
Would this Martyr die in vain?

Crucified on either side,
One held scorn, the Lord decried,
But the other hope portrayed;
Prayer is heard and Christ replied!
While there is a hope in Heaven,
Pleading souls are not denied!

Love predominant this day,
Faithful friends stand near the Lord;
Jesus shouts from His rude cross:
'It is finished!' Love outpoured
Has fulfilled Redemption's Plan:
Death is vanquished! Praise the LORD!

SCRIPTURE IN SONG

The horror, pathos, grief, yet power of the sacrifice of **JESUS** on that Roman raised cross on Calvary, never dims as those who seek to know the depths of its meaning in today's world, come to faith, realising His power to save—to cleanse by the purity of His blood and the gifting of His Life for ALL who trust.

127. CALVARY
Luke 23:33–49. Tune: *St Margaret* (Repeat 3rd line 8.8.8.6.

Christ's cross was borne to Calvary;
The Lord of Life was called to die!
He gave His Live for you and me,
The King born to be Man.

His cross was meant for you and me,
That scaffold raised on Calvary;
He came to set the prisoner free,
Redeemer, Friend, and Guide.

His cross was meant for Calvary:
A dying thief put in his plea
And Jesus gave him hope that day,
The Saviour of the world.

His cross enhances Calvary
For it became the place where we
May come, receive His pardon free,
Jesus, Eternal Lord!

Christ's cross was raised for humankind:
So all the world may now be free;
It is our gift to choose His Way,
For Christ now offers Life today!

SCRIPTURE IN SONG

The Faith Community has received the Gospel of the **RESURRECTION** with joy and their lives have been transformed, by the power of the Risen Lord. This is why the Good News has been translated into song countless times— to proclaim its truth! To the faithful, the Gospel has retained its wonder!

128. RISE THE SUN IN RADIANT SPLENDOUR

John 20:1–18. Tune: *Austria* 8.7.8.7.D. Trochaic

Rise the sun in radiant splendour,
Clothe the sky in peerless blue,
Dress the world in shining garments,
Celebrate a Dawn that's new!
Never has there been rejoicing
Such as this that greets the dawn:
Christ has risen, Hallelujah!
All the world may be reborn!

Claim the dawn! Its light resplendent
Greets the valley of despair,
Where a garden, spring clad garden,
Waits its glorious news to share.
Rock is rending, burst asunder:
Death cannot its Victim hold.
Christ has risen, Hallelujah!
Jesus' friends find Joy unfold!

Morning breaks on visions splendid,
Gilded colours paint the Earth;
A new day has dawned upon us:
Day of grace, the day for faith!
Hope has come that knows no ending,
Opening to Eternity.
Christ has risen, Hallelujah!
All the world may now go free!

SCRIPTURE IN SONG

MARY MAGDALENE had announced the news to Jesus' friends on resurrection morning. John and Peter had confirmed the first sighting: 'Jesus is Alive!' What happened when closed doors no longer mattered to Jesus can immediately portray the fact that He was seen no longer wearing Earth's soil!

129. PEACE BE WITH YOU
John 20:19-29. Tune: *Saved by Grace* L.M.

He came to them in twilight's hour,
His radiance filled the room with light;
When Jesus stood among His friends,
He spoke His blessing to each heart.

CHORUS
'Let peace be yours as dawn returns,
And peace attends the noonday heat;
May peace remain in evening hours,
My peace, surround you through the night.'

Their fears were great, they'd hid from view,
Christ knew His friends, their desperate plight;
The doors were locked, yet here He was!
He stood with them, His wounds in view.

'Receive My Spirit,' Jesus said,
'As I was sent, I send in might!'
He breathed on them the Breath of God:
His Spirit gave them strength that night.

As joy erupted in the room,
Their faith returned and fear took flight!
The Lord commissioned them to spread
His News: 'Go now, reveal God's Light!'

SCRIPTURE IN SONG

That trudging along the road to **EMMAUS** following the crucifixion of Jesus was indeed a dreadful dirge until the Stranger/Friend came into step with them. It is this writer's contention that the people concerned were Cleopas, and his wife who had stood at the cross!!! See Luke 24:18, with John 19:25. In their home, sorrow turned into joyful praise. And so, it always will!

130. THE EMMAUS ROAD
Luke 24::13-35.   Tune: *Vox Dilecti*   D.C.M.

They walked that day along the road
To hopeless thoughts resigned,
For sadness claimed their converse there,
Dark Calvary on their mind.

CHORUS
Come, stay with us, abide with us,
The night is hastening on;
Remain with us and guide us, Lord,
Till travelling days are done.

And then He came, He counselled them;
They thought their hearts would rend!
The Scriptures had foretold a day
Where death is not the end!

He reasoned there that God so loved
The world, He gave His Son,
That all may walk the Upward Path
And find God's Kingdom won.

He made as though He would go on,
As they came home to rest;
But needing still His presence there,
They bid Him be their Guest.

He entered then and sat with them,
He blessed their daily bread;
They saw His hands, those nail-print scars,
'It is the Lord!' they said.

SCRIPTURE IN SONG

This is, indeed a "hymn" of Redemption: that of **PETER**! Peter's natural sorrow at the crucifixion of his Lord was compounded by the wretchedness of his failure that night in the Judgement Hall! He needed help, and it came! Jesus chose that morning on the beach in Galilee. Did Peter love his old life more than the New Life Jesus offered? The answer is in his ready response!

131. DO YOU LOVE ME?

John 21:1–23.   Tune: *Blessed Assurance*   9.9.9.9.D.

'Come from your toiling, in from the sea,
Come and now bring the griefs that you bear;
Come from your trials, those waves of despair,
Come to Me, rest, unburden your care.'

CHORUS
*You know I'll follow! Lord, You can tell
I am Your friend, and I'll walk with You;
Be my Companion down the long years,
Guide me each day till Heaven's in view.*

'Say, do you love me more than all these—
Things that would bind you close to the Earth?
Love has its reasons, wherever cast,
What are your values? What is of worth?

'Share all your longings as we converse,
I have supplied your needs for each day;
Share with Me now your aims and desires,
Do you intend My word to obey?

'Stir up the coals, rekindle the flame,
Find your vocation, pastor My sheep;
Shepherd My lambs, or they'll go astray,
Lead them to safety, the path is steep.

'You're My disciples, learning from Me,
Finding your faith in God's precious word;
Time now has come to share what you've seen,
Time for declaring what you have heard.'

SCRIPTURE IN SONG

The writings of Luke, the doctor who gave medical care and continuing support to Paul during his missionary journeys and imprisonments, are said to be some of the greatest documents of the 1st century! Here, his news can turn to a song—it is a hymn—the Good News: "Jesus is **ASCENDED** into Heaven!" Can you *hear* the disciples singing this hymn? Let it be yours also!

132. GOOD NEWS!
Luke 24:45-53. Tune: *Amazing Grace* C.M.

The news is out! The Lord is raised!
Tes, Jesus lives today;
He came to us, He walks with us,
He gives us hope this day!

The news is great! The Lord's alive:
He left the tomb—God's Day;
With tender love, He brings His peace,
And near us He will stay!

The news is true: Christ Jesus lives!
He walks our road today;
Our needs are met, our burdens eased,
He's with us as we pray!

The news is ours: we claim His power;
He lives, our Lord, today!
Ascended to The Father now,
His purpose will hold sway.

This news is yours, so trust Him now,
The Lord gives Life today!
Believe His word and be set free
To live for Him each day.

..... oOo .....

PART FOUR

THE GOSPEL IN ACTION

The cross stands empty on its hill!
Our resurrected Lord, the Bearer of Eternal Life,
commissions His Disciples to become Apostles.
They would take the Gospel to the world
IN THE POWER OF THE HOLY SPIRIT!

THE GOSPEL IN ACTION

FROM JERUSALEM TO THE WORLD

THE CROSS-BOUND WAY

The *Ruach*—the **Holy Spirit**—has been active in the world from the commencement of Creation: before Pentecost, moving **UPON** the patriarchs and the prophets, invigorating them to act—take hold of God's word, let it be heard. From the Day of Pentecost, God's people have known the **INDWELLING** Spirit, empowering us to proclaim, to live, **the Gospel—the Good News**!

Peter, Andrew, James, and John, all the apostles, were joined by Paul and friends to carry the Good News of how Jesus came to save the lost and change the world: *TO THE WORLD*!

SCRIPTURE IN SONG

In opening the pages of The Acts of The Apostles, we have come to a new phase in the singing of the Good News! Again, the writer is Dr Luke. The hymns of the past journeys through the Old and New Testaments became the "overture" to a great symphony: **PENTECOST** is the precursor to Christianity!

133. PENTECOST

Genesis 1:1–2, Acts 2.   Tune: *Come ye thankful people* 7.7.7.7. D.

Wonderful! God's mighty power:
Dawning Light on Earth's first hour;
His great Spirit breathed upon
Ocean depths and life was born!

CHORUS
Holy Spirit, breathe in me,
Make me all I ought to be;
For my darkness, shine Your Light,
For my weakness, grant Your might.

Awesome is the Spirit's power,
Through the years, at every hour
Breathing insights of the Lord,
As recorded in God's word.

Energising, holy power,
Strength was given for the hour;
In God's time, His Spirit came,
Bearing Pentecostal Flame.

Life transforming, Spirit power,
Make me ready for this hour;
Holy Spirit, move in me,
Fit me for Eternity.

SCRIPTURE IN SONG

Now, here is something to sing about! The first crumbling of national and racial borders is seen as **PHILIP** meets up with an Ethiopian in the employ of royalty, has the joy of opening the Scriptures, and presents the Gospel—Jesus!

134. SEEKING TRUTH
Acts 8:26–40. Tune: *Troyte* 8.8.8.4.

I sought for Truth in Scripture's page,
Turned to the ancient prophet sage
That spoke of One in future age,
Who Truth would bear.

I sought for Truth in parchments rare;
They spoke of Him with reverent care;
And, as I read, I saw Him there
Who lived the Truth.

I sought for Truth at Jesus' feet,
And He revealed the Source of Light;
There, as I pondered life complete,
I knew the Truth.

His promise is, 'Now come to Me,
You'll know the Truth, you shall be free;
Receive My words, believe in Me,
Know Truth indeed!'

I found the Truth and I was free,
Free from the doubts that hindered me;
Now I may live eternally,
For Christ IS Truth!

SCRIPTURE IN SONG

PETER found it difficult to reach out beyond his natural frame of reference. He was a Jew, still bound to the culture he knew and loved. It took a dramatic episode to shake him out of the past, into the wider world that was beckoning. He had already moved out as far as Joppa. No further was he prepared to go! Then came the challenge! With much "nudging", Peter finally said, *YES*!

135. FAITH'S CHALLENGE
Acts 10.   Tune: *Vox Dilecti*   D.C.M.

I come before You, LORD, today
To worship in this place;
I wait to know Your will, O LORD,
For You to plan my days.
I enter now with waiting heart:
Your Spirit calls me near.
In holding fast Your promises,
I claim Your presence here.

I know not what the future holds,
Nor yet what need demands;
I would not faint before the task,
My times are in Your hands.
Now, by Your grace, I pledge to serve
Throughout life's busy day;
And here I bring life's offering:
To love You and obey.

A pilgrim, on the Road of Life,
I make this sacred vow.
That I may bear the strain of toil,
O grant Your blessing now.
LORD, tread the onward way with me
As I the challenge dare;
I place my life, my strength, my all,
Into Your loving care.

SCRIPTURE IN SONG

Observe the people who comprised the leader team in the Church at Antioch—here, first known as **CHRISTIANS**. In this group were the men who would embark on the very first missionary journey. Saul became known as Paul! Do take note that the Church was comprised of Jews, Africans, and a man who had grown up with Herod! It is good reason for a hymn to be sung!

136. HAVE YOU DECIDED?
Acts 13:1. Tune: *Maryland* (with chorus. D.L.M.

Have you decided what to do
With all your aims and energy?
The rest of life now beckons you,
And Jesus calls you to His Way.

CHORUS
'Come, come to Me,' the Saviour calls,
'So weary from your yesterdays;
Come now with Me to find release,
Come, walk My Road and learn My ways.'

Have you remembered what the cost
To bring to view Eternity?
Have you now seen the cross-road sign
That marks the way to Calvary?

Have you considered what you'll do
To ease the burdens of this world?
Christ spreads His challenge out to you;
He has a task to which you're called.

I have decided what to do
With all my aims and energy:
The rest of life now beckons me
As Jesus calls me to His Way!

SCRIPTURE IN SONG

SAUL, the character first met in Acts where he was pleased to see those who followed Jesus' teaching stoned to death, has undergone such a dramatic transformation that not only has his name changed to **PAUL**, but his work! Paul commences missionary endeavour and speaks the Gospel in his letters!

137. FAITH'S VISION
Acts 13:1, Romans 5:1-5, 8:28. Tune: *Simeon* L.M.

Faith brings the ample evidence
Of boundless things not seen or heard
For, with the eyes and ears of faith,
Our inner sense of faith is stirred.

Faith brings ability to trust
Though clouds obscure the path ahead;
Its vision sees, beyond the night,
That Light will dawn and doubt be dead.

Faith brings assurances that all
The promises of God are real,
The promise known, the promise claimed;
Such gifting will God's grace reveal.

Faith brings the access into grace
Wherein we stand and we rejoice
In hope of all God's glory now;
His love outpoured brings heartfelt peace.

Faith brings the knowledge that all things
Will work together for the good,
The ultimate great vict'ry, of
All those whose trust is in God's word.

SCRIPTURE IN SONG

As a young assistant, known in Acts as **JOHN MARK**, this young man failed as a missionary but, at last, he earned Paul's approval and respect. This comforting news is found in Paul's 2nd Letter to Timothy. Mark comes HOME.

138. TAKE HEART, BE STRONG!
Acts 13:1–13, 2 Timothy 4:11.   Tune: *Spohr*   8.6.8.6.8.6.

Take heart, fear not, be strong, believe
That Jesus gave His life
To send our sins to waiting tombs
Within the depths of Earth.
He came to bring new hope to all;
Through Him, we truly live.

The way ahead seems dark at times:
I seek the road to tread.
Where is the path that seemed so bright?
That "signpost" up ahead
Reveals the Cross Road, and my Lord:
By His own hand I'm led!

Why is the strength of vibrant faith
So vital to our cause?
And, why the emphasis on grace
Today? It is because
These are the gifts of God; take hold,
They will fulfil God's cause.

In Jesus Crist we place our trust;
In Him resides all Truth!
Believe His word, discover faith,
Here trust displays its worth.
By standing on God's promises,
We know Eternal Life!

SCRIPTURE IN SONG

THE ACTS OF THE APOSTLES—the book relating to the written records of the amazing spread of the Gospel through what was then the Roman Empire—could be appropriately titled **THE ACTS OF THE HOLY SPIRIT**! This song is one of "global" testimony for Greeks, Asians, Africans, even some Romans, were receiving and accepting the Gospel of Jesus' saving grace!

139. ALIVE IN CHRIST
Acts of the Apostles.   Tune: *Mozart*   8.8.8.8.8.8. Iambic

Now made alive, though we were dead,
Walking sin's way, kin of the world;
But God is rich in mercy free:
In wondrous love, His Son involved—
When we were dead, He raised us up:
We are alive in Jesus Christ!

Exceeding rich, God's grace to us;
His kindness shown in Christ, His Son;
It is by grace that we are saved
Through faith alive, His gift alone.
Created new, we trust in Him:
We are made free in Jesus Christ!

Strangers we were, and alien souls,
Having no hope or life in God;
But now, in Christ, we are at-one,
Washed in His flowing, precious Blood!
He is our peace, we rest in Him:
We are made new in Jesus Christ!

Strangers no more, and far from home,
No more alone, we live in Him!
Our fellowship His Spirit seals
As worthy citizens of Heav'n:
We now are formed His "temple" here:
We are made whole in Jesus Christ!

SCRIPTURE IN SONG

Here is Paul's great statement of faith to the **ROMANS**. It flows into a song:

140. THERE IS NO CONDEMNATION

Romans 8:1–27.   Tune: *Rutherford*   7.6.7.6. D. Iambic

There is no condemnation
For those in Jesus Christ;
Through Him, God's Holy Spirit
Has set us free to trust!
We do not live the world's way,
We are aligned to grace;
Our minds are on His motives,
Our hearts know life and peace.

We're led by God's own Spirit,
We are His children dear,
We ask our "Abba", Father,
To cast aside our fear!
The Holy Spirit counsels
That we are heirs with Christ
For, if we share His suff'ring,
Also, we'll share His best.

All wait in expectation
To see God's glory rise;
For any present burdens
Cannot outweigh His grace.
And all creation waits yet
To overcome decay,
While we await redemption
To the Eternal Day.

Our hope is without measure,
And unconfined God's aid;
His Spirit helps our weakness,
He prays at God's own side!
What, then, are our responses?
If God is for us, none,
No, none can overcome us:
We praise what He has done!

SCRIPTURE IN SONG

Paul's great statement of faith continues into a 2nd song. His testimony of faith reaches a climax here which requires a culminating focus. Let faith sing!

141. WE KNOW!
Romans 8:28–39.   Tune: *Penlan*   7.6.7.6. D. Iambic

We know that all things work now,
Together for the good
Of those who truly love Him,
Our great, Eternal God.
According to His purpose
Before all time began,
He moulds us in the likeness
Of Jesus Christ, His Son.

And, who can separate us
From Christ, our Living Lord?
Shall hardship, tribulation,
Shall peril, or the sword?
Jesus is interceding
Before the Throne of Grace;
He stands at God's right hand and,
Through Him, we find our peace.

In all things, ours the vict'ry!
We're more than conquerors
Through Jesus Christ who loves us;
No one can sever us!
I am convinced that nothing,
No creature ever could
Detach us from God's loving
In Jesus Christ, our Lord!

SCRIPTURE IN SONG

There are, perhaps, no better words to describe the true nature of love than Paul's great "Love Song" in **CORINTHIANS** as transposed now in this Hymn and written so that, among other settings, it may be used as a wedding song.

142. A WEDDING PRAYER

I Corinthians 13. Tune: *St Margaret* 8.8.8.8.6.

O Lord of Love, today we pray
Your blessing give, so rich and free:
Our friends have come their vows to pay
And, in their love, to ask that You
Will guide through all their way.

Lord, You have taught us love is kind,
Patient, enduring, suff'ring long;
No evil thought ensnares the mind
When love does keep no score of wrong;
Such love as one will bind.

True love, it's known, will never fail,
It bears all things, its hope is sure;
Though knowledge won't always avail—
We know in part—we do know that
The perfect will not fail.

We see today through clouded glass,
But, one day, face to Face with You;
While life shall last, please bless our days.
There now abides faith, hope, and love:
The greatest: love! We praise.

Now set Your seal upon this love,
A union fixed before You now;
Lord, You once came Your love to prove
And called us to abide in You:
Abide with us in Love.

SCRIPTURE IN SONG

THE FRUIT OF THE SPIRIT should be seen in the subject matter somewhat hidden by the text of **GALATIANS**. the truth of it is this: There are 9 types of fruit: the 1st 3 relate to our relationship with God: *love, joy, peace*; the 2nd 3 relate to our relationship with others: *patience, kindness, goodness*; and the 3rd 3 relate to our relationship with ourselves: faithfulness, gentleness, and self-control. It is time to partake of this fruit: *all* are available!!!

143. THE FRUIT OF THE SPIRIT
Galatians 5: 22–23, Ephesians 3:14–19. Tune: *Arizona* L.M.

God has a plan for this, my life:
I am to grow rich fruit for Him.
And, also for all others' gain;
Yes! I must grow fruit that is prime.

God has a purpose for my life,
Grow Holy Spirit fruit! Behold:
Love, joy, peace; patience, kindness, worth;
Be faithful, gentle, self-controlled.

This is God's purpose for my life:
Grow deep, grow up, grow tall as meant,
Each branch to spread and grow good fruit,
Relying on divine intent.

From the beginning, God's great Plan:
Before all ages had begun
He knew my name, what I'd become!
O LORD, fulfil Your perfect Plan.

The Fruit of God's own Spirit will
Bring blessing to a people that
Know nothing of His love, joy, peace:
O may this fruit be found complete.

SCRIPTURE IN SONG

Paul's letter to the **EPHESIANS** soars to the heights of encouragement for the Church. The first chapter contains 3 great promises: **We <u>have</u>:** Redemption —through the Blood of Jesus, an incorruptible inheritance—for God is our Father, and the gift of the Holy Spirit—the "foretaste" of what will be ours! Also, Paul brings the nations together: GRACE—Gentiles, PEACE: Israel!

144. GRACE AND PEACE

Ephesians 1:1–14. Tune: *Jesus, Tender Shepherd* 8.7.8.7. Trochaic

Grace and peace have come from Heaven:
Jesus Christ will keep the soul
Faithful to the living word, and
Holy, for He makes us whole.

Praise is offered to the Saviour,
Who is all our heart's delight;
He has chosen us to be now
Holy, blameless, in His sight.

Chosen from before creation,
He predestined us to be
Members of His own dear fam'ly,
Holy, by His grace now free!

Grace and peace are flowing freely
From the very Throne of God:
Grace to conquer in the combat,
Peace to grant the soul's true good.

Ours to know redemption's grace for
By His Blood He cleansed from sin!
Our inheritance He purchased,
By His Spirit, we will win!

SCRIPTURE IN SONG

Paul's letters to the Church in the many areas of Europe and Asia are predominant throughout the New Testament. His counsel to the **EPHESIANS** is truly superb! His words of praise will find responding melodies in the soul!

145. THE FAMILY OF GOD
Ephesians 3:14–21. Tune: *Beethoven* L.M.

We are the family of God!
We have derived our name from Christ;
His name is written on our heart,
And in His riches, we are bless'd.

The Spirit comes, empowering us;
Within our inner life is peace,
For Christ now dwells within our heart:
By faith He nurtures us in grace.

Now we have found the "living tree",
The faith that finds its deepest root
In fertile ground to nourish love;
We find our strength in precious fruit.

LORD, we are finding, by Your grace,
How deep and high, how wide, and long,
The love of Christ! It reaches us!
And, all Your fulness is our song!

We know, dear LORD, in love You grant
Immeasurably more for us—
Beyond all that we ask, or think!
Your power's at work through all our days!

In Christ, we have found access to
Your Throne: a confidence, by faith,
To seek Your aid, Your guidance, and
Your grace, rejoicing in Your worth!

SCRIPTURE IN SONG

Paul. having been schooled in the ways set down in the Old Testament, needed a dramatic transformation of his soul in order to change his outlook from LAW to GRACE. His on-going walk with Jesus, through the power of the Holy Spirit, enabled him to understand and to exemplify the way of holiness. He has expressed it all so well in **EPHESIANS**:

146. HOLINESS IN THE EVERY DAY

Ephesians 4:1–16. Tune: *Morning Hymn* L.M.

These are the marks of holiness:
Humility and gentleness,
And patience born with each in love:
These are the signs of Christ-likeness.

Baptised with Fire; He has, in might,
Set all our hearts aflame for Him:
The Fire—the Holy Spirit—comes
To energise and vict'ry win.

We have been cleansed by holy Fire,
Refined within His furnaces.
By faith made bold and free from sin,
The LORD now sanctifies our days.

He calls us to a servant-path
So that God's people may be bless'd
And reach a unity of faith,
Mature, and made complete in Christ.

Our one true hope is Jesus Christ:
One LORD, one Faith, one Cleansing: His!
One God and Father of us all,
He's over all, He's ALL in all!

SCRIPTURE IN SONG

Paul was always walking under the watchful eyes of Roman soldiers, often under guard! Their **ARMOUR** surmounted the clothing of these men and Paul came to see that there was a spiritual application to the apparel of his guards!

147. PUT ON THE CHRISTIAN ARMOUR
Ephesians 6:10–20. Tune: *Duke Street* L.M.

Put on the Armour of the LORD,
So you may stand firm, hold no flaws;
Our struggle's not in Earth's vain wars,
We fight the Saviour's worthy cause.

Stand firm in Christ, and buckle on
The Belt of Truth: it will secure
The whole: with this, you'll win the fight;
Truth stands the test! You will endure!

Let Righteousness secure your heart,
On this your life will now depend!
The Gospel of His Peace proclaim,
Prepare to march through ev'ry land.

Take up the Shield of Faith, be strong!
No matter where the arrow flies,
All evil will be thwarted by
A Faith that is alive and wise.

Let ev'ry thought of Jesus' Blood
And His great grace now be your guard;
The Helmet of Salvation wear
And take the Spirit's Sword: God's word!

Now be at prayer; stand watch each day:
Request the LORD to fuel your zest
To share Good News, proclaim God's word:
The "mystery" made known in Christ.

THE PSALM OF PAUL

Paul's 2nd chapter to the **PHILIPPIANS** is thought by many to be one of the hymns of the Early Church. Possibly true, it is set, and sounds like a "psalm"!

148. THE EXAMPLE OF JESUS

Philippians 2:1–11. Tune: *He Leadeth Me*   L.M.

Here is the great encouragement
To be united now with Christ;
This is the comfort of His love,
The fellowship of lives so bless'd.

CHORUS
So that all joy should be complete,
Unite your mind with Jesus' goal;
Reflect His own exampled love
Be one in purpose, pure and whole.

Have no ambition trained on self,
No vain conceit, no false renown;
Consider others more the bless'd:
Look to their interests, not your own.

So, let your attitude be like
The attitude of Christ, our Lord;
In nature, He's unique with God:
He came to us to live God's word.

He knew the path of servanthood,
He came to be like us so that
We all could be like unto Him:
He went to Calvary for that!

Therefore, He is exalted now
We will proclaim that Christ is Lord
Confessing His transcendent fame,
And glorify our Father, God.

SCRIPTURE IN SONG

Paul was eager to impress the value of prayer and the Christian's walk in the community upon the **COLOSSIANS**. His counsel came via a letter of grace!

149. PRAYER AND PERSEVERANCE

Colossians, selected.   Tune: *Belmont*   C.M.

The strength God gives is found through prayer;
Be watchful, thankful, too,
And pray that God will open doors
To share Good News so true!

Once you were dead in sin, but now:
You are alive in Christ!
Redeemed, renewed to live for Him,
Let no one judge the least!

Now, make the most of everything:
Be wise, be kind, and true.
Let all your words be full of grace;
Be fair in all your do.

Put on the garments of God's grace:
Be kind, forbear, forgive,
And, let the peace of God enfold
You in His loving care.

To be the Lord's ambassador,
Stand firm within His will,
With faith now made secure,
Your promises fulfil.

In all your daily tasks, be whole!
In all you are, be true;
You witness for the Lord you love,
His grace accompanies you.

SCRIPTURE IN SONG

Paul's two letters to the **THESSALONIANS** are marked by his emphatic teaching concerning Jesus' Second Coming—indeed, a foreword to John's epic "The Apocalypse". Paul's counsel on the subject is here transposed as a song:

150. THE WORLD TO COME
1st Thess. 4:13–5:28, 2nd Thess. 1 –2. Tune: *Armadale* L.M.

We find, within the Word of Life,
The news that Christ will come again.
His Kingdom will be then installed
Throughout the Earth; He comes to reign!

We're not as those who have no hope,
Our trust is in the Lord of Life,
For we believe that Jesus died
To save us, cleanse us, from sin's strife.

The dead in Christ will then be raised,
To live eternally, in Heav'n.
The time of His appearing is
Not known but be alert for Him.

While in this "Day of Grace", keep watch,
Be patient, comforting, and kind
To those, the weak, the troubled, lost.
And, be at peace, rejoicing find.

In everything give thanks; hold fast
To that which is for good of all;
Your spirit, mind, and body be
Preserved blameless unto His Call.

The Lord is faithful and He will
Bring all these things to pass in time.
When time becomes Eternity,
The Lord will come to take us "Home".

SCRIPTURE IN SONG

Throughout his ministry, Paul called Christ's followers, both corporately and personally, to faithfulness. Here, his words to **TIMOTHY** are set as a song.

151. THE CALL TO FAITHFULNESS
2 Timothy 2:11-13. Tune: *Maidstone* 7.7.7.7. D.

Wonderful, God's faithfulness!
Ever present with His care,
When the day is dark indeed,
I have found Him to be there.
God has called to faithfulness
All the days of pilgrimage;
Echo of His faith in me,
Faith is found to serve this age.

Steadfast is God's faithfulness!
Though I might His will defy,
Still His faithfulness remains:
God will not Himself deny!
God has called me to be true
All the days of pilgrimage;
He's invested faith in me:
I will serve in this, our age.

Trusting in God's faithfulness,
There is hope for what's to be;
Standing on His promises,
Faith in action strengthens me.
God has called me to this hope
All the days of pilgrimage;
He has found in me a faith
That will stand in this our age!

SCRIPTURE IN SONG

Paul's words to **TITUS**, whom he treated as a son, are couched in terms of counsel. He was a young man already engaged in missionary endeavour. Paul urges him to "adorn the doctrine". Titus was encouraged to "speak the things that pertain to sound doctrine." He was to be sure of his faith, and preach it!

152. THE GOSPEL: GOOD NEWS!
Titus, chapter 2. Tune: *Coronation* 8.6.8.6.8.6.

Christ died because of human sin,
According to God's word;
He died upon a cross of shame,
For us He shed His blood.
The third day, He was raised to life:
He is the Son of God!

Too long, the world has passed Him by,
Believing not the Man;
Eternal life was promised from
Before the world began.
In due time Jesus came to save
This weary world from sin.

The Truth must now be heard by all!
Yes! To the pure, all things
Are pure, the world avows the wrong—
From commoners to kings!
The Gospel News must now be heard:
Around the world the Good News rings!

Adorn the doctrine of the LORD,
His Truth portray, by word
And deed. Preach: pointing to the hope
Of Christ's return, and gird
Yourself to live via Spirit power:
The LORD will know your worth.

SCRIPTURE IN SONG

Who wrote **HEBREWS**? Apollos? Barnabas? Paul? The style is not Paul's. This is a major theological treatise—Paul tended to give guidance for daily living. Paul could have "guided" this letter, though anonymously (Jewish leaders would not tolerate his work to Jewish Christians), via his erudite aide, Dr Luke.

153. THE LIVING WORD
Hebrews 1. Tune: *Wareham* L.M.

In times gone by, the LORD declared
His word through prophets once inspired;
Down through the years, in various ways,
His Voice was clear, His news desired.

There came a day, In God's own time,
When He redeemed us through His Son
Jesus, Creator, Heir of all:
By Him the darkest night is gone!

Jesus, the Son, the radiance
Of God's own glory, came to Earth;
He is the One who has revealed
God's likeness, though of humble birth.

Sustaining all things by His word,
He came to make us whole and clean!
He sits enthroned, the Lord of Life,
Beside the Majesty of Heav'n.

His throne will last forever, and
His royal sceptre will defend;
He rules by grace in righteousness,
His tide of years will never end.

Jesus, the Christ, Anointed One,
The source of joy! We will exclaim:
The garments of the Earth will fade,
But He remains, ever the same!

SCRIPTURE IN SONG

HEBREWS, in just one verse, takes hold of the power of prayer: *Let us therefore come boldly unto the Throne of Grace, that we may obtain mercy, and find grace to help in time of need.* MERCY is given to those who deserve God's favour; GRACE, unbounded grace, is available to all who do not deserve it!

154. GRACE AND MERCY
Hebrews 4:16. Tune: *Rest* 8.6.8.8.6.

I come into Your Presence, Lord,
In awe of Your great Name.
You hear my faintest whisper, Lord,
I trust Your liberating word;
Redeeming grace, I claim.

When shadows on my path appear,
Yet I will sing Your praise,
For I will find You always near.
You walk with me and, oh, so dear:
The radiance of Your face.

When cherished dreams lie shattered here,
O Lord, You counsel me;
You challenge me to trust Your care,
And, in Your strength, my all to dare;
Your mercy is my plea.

You took my sadness, sorrow's tide,
Releasing grief to grace!
The brokenness I could not hide
Is healed, restored, by love supplied!
Your gentle touch brings peace.

When danger threatens, help is near:
Your promises are true!
Your are my Hope, I shall not fear.
My faith is firm: Lord, You are here
And You make all things new!

SCRIPTURE IN SONG

HEBREWS, the anonymous book, speaks the Gospel to the heart of Israel. Tutored by the peerless Gamaliel in the Temple school, Paul could have dictated these chapters to a scribe, though the language flows in another's style. Was his hand upon it? Most think not. Maybe, it was the erudite Apollos, well-schooled in the history of Israel. The work is magnificent, particularly the chapter devoted to the Faith we hold, transposed in song:

155. FAITH IS THE EVIDENCE
Hebrews, 11. Tune: *Ten thousand souls* D.C.M.

Faith is the vital evidence
Of things not seen or heard;
Trust grants the true assurance of
God's plan for which all yearned.

We see the glorious cross, and hear
The Gospel News today,
Yet there is much for us to learn:
Our faith will lead the way!

This record of the ages past
Reveals the history of
The hopeful men of old who held
To faith: they knew God's love!

The precious promises of God
Held hope for Abraham
And all who lived their faith each day:
They knew *Messiah* would come!

The faithful men of old held trust,
Though all was not fulfilled.
God planned the wondrous Ultimate:
There's hope for all the world!

SCRIPTURE IN SONG

JAMES has brought us to the penultimate section of Scripture: that of the **GENERAL EPISTLES**. Who was James? The brother of John? No, he had been assassinated! The Epistle of James was, in all probability, written by the brother of Jesus! What a transforming view of the resurrected Lord can do! James became the leader of the Church in Jerusalem and his words were directed to the Jewish diaspora: those scattered abroad through the nations.

156. STAND THE TEST!
James 1. Tune: *Arizona* L.M.

Don't be surprised! Count it all joy,
Yes, when you are perplexed! It is
When trouble comes, endurance finds
That it can put on strength through grace.

Don't be perturbed! Though trials invade,
These are the means where faith can stand
The test. So, face those troubles, smile!
You'll be completed by God's hand.

Don't think of failure! Realize
Your doubts recede as wisdom looms;
Our God is generous, and cares;
He listens to faith's prayer: He comes!

Don't be a waverer, like waves
Upon a storm-tossed sea! Know this:
God blesses those enduring trials
And, afterward, life's crown is yours!

Don't be misled! The Gospel News
Is this: all that is good for needs
Comes to us from our Father, God:
There are no shadows where He treads!

SCRIPTURE IN SONG

PETER also "sang his psalms"! The **GENERAL EPISTLES** do not pass him by! Peter found his love again! His ministry was one of faithfulness, unto death! A man of action, not often focussed on parchment, but his words stand today!

157. CHRIST'S EXAMPLE
1 Peter 1:13–23. Tune: *Saved by Grace* D.L.M.

Prepare your mind for Jesus Christ,
Be self-controlled, and set your heart
Upon the grace that's given you
As Christ reveals the life "apart"!

CHORUS:
Just as the Lord lived holiness,
So set your heart on holy ways,
For it is written in God's word,
Live holiness the Lord to please.

Do not conform to worldly ways,
Obedience, your chosen path;
Since you now call upon the Lord,
Now live your life: be pure in heart.

It is not gold, which perishes,
That has redeemed us unto God,
Nor heritage that keeps us whole:
It is by Jesus' precious blood!

He was the Lamb without a stain,
No defect could be found in Him;
This was God's Plan to make us whole
Before the world was set in time.

We have been born again to live,
Our faith and hope are in the Lord!
Be purified and live in love
Through the enduring Son of God.

SCRIPTURE IN SONG

PETER, in his 2nd Letter to the Church, emphasises the imperative for Christians to be aware of the urgency of proclaiming the Gospel *TODAY!* The world's "dark night" is hastening on. The Lord needs His ambassadors today!

158. CALLED TO THE HOUR

2 Peter 1:1–11. Tune: *Ten thousand Souls* D.C.M.

The Lord has called us to this hour,
And we would seek His Face,
That we may speak our soul's desire
Within this holy place.
We seek both grace and peace to live;
The precious faith we hold
Must be proclaimed! Yes, make it known!
God's power will make us bold.

Having escaped from sin's dark night,
Add to your faith: virtue,
And, to your knowledge: uprightness.
To patience: love that's due!
In all things, now be kind for, if
These gifts should now abound,
Your knowledge of the Lord shall grow:
You'll spread Good News around!

A Light to pierce this world's dark night
Of sin and deep despair,
Is newly kindled as we pledge
The Gospel to declare!
Now, in obedience to God's Call,
Good News to gladly bear,
Lord, lead us into all the world,
The Living Word to share.

SCRIPTURE IN SONG

JOHN is credited with 3 Letters, set in the **GENERAL EPISTLES**. But John did not sign his name! The author's identity has been solidified after long years. The Church Fathers: Irenaeus, Clement, Tertullian, and Origen, provided undeniable evidence that John bar Zebedee put his "pen" to paper for the project! But who was John, really? He was the cousin of Jesus! They would have played together, at times, as children having grown up in the north!

159. BOUNDLESS LOVE!
1, 2, 3 John, selected.   Tune: *Dennis* S.M.

How great the love of God!
It reaches even me?
How could it be, He cares for me?
He reigns eternally!

The love of God, beyond
Degree: it's boundless, free;
The world is in the Hands of God?
Such love, how can it be?

God's love was found throughout
The ages past; and now
It is discerned in Jesus Christ:
He came LIFE to endow!

And, how should we respond
To love outpoured today?
In love, the Sinless Son gave all:
His death grants LIFE to me!

The world must know that love
Displayed on Calvary:
This is a task for me to take:
LORD: grant me power today.

THE PSALM OF JOHN

THE PSALM OF JOHN provides this rare occurrence of New Testament poetry. The Hebraic source is clearly seen although it is here transposed into the rhyme and rhythm of the English form of poetic nuance. The theme of love is paramount. John's words bring hope to both the young and the mature.

160. SUPREME LOVE
1 John 2:12–14. Tune: *Rockingham* L.M.

This news is for God's Family,
It is Good News of sins forgiv'n:
"For God so loved the world, He gave
His only Son; by Him, LIFE'S giv'n."

Although still new to Bible Truth,
Though young in faith, your battle's won:
The evil one no longer rules!
You live for Christ, praise what He's done.

All the mature in faith today
Have held the word of God in love;
The history of ages past
Resound in you: God's love you prove!

Existing from before all time
Began upon Creation's Day,
Jesus, Eternal Lord, became
The Son who died on Calvary.

He lives today for you and me;
He calls us all to live in love
For all God's children, all the world,
That all may know Eternal Life.

SCRIPTURE IN SONG

JOHN pronounces, for all to hear, the **LOVE OF GOD** and our responding love for Him. It's not his final word though–this will be the culminating book of the Bible. We focus now on John's over-riding message for the Church: L.O.V.E.!

161. HOW GREAT THE LOVE OF GOD
1 John 3. Tune: *He Wipes the Tear* (with chorus.   D.L.M.

How great the love of God to us:
He knows no boundaries on Earth!
The depth of His great love is known
To all who recognise its worth.
God's love ensures we've moved from death,
And living now, eternal life!
God showed us, in His Act of Love,
Christ Jesus came His love to prove.

How strong the love of God for us:
All evil bows to His command
And those accepting of His love,
Will conquer sin by trusting Him.
Our love is for each other now:
We know true love—it is of God!
We are prepared to stand up for
All those in need and give them aid.

How mighty is the love of God!
Speak love, give witness, and obey,
Our actions show what we hold dear;
Our deeds determine what we say.
So! Come with confidence to God,
Be bold in what you ask of Him:
You will receive all that you need.
Love one another, all: for Him!

SCRIPTURE IN SONG

JUDE provides the **BENEDICTION**, not only for the **GENERAL EPISTLES** but also for the Christian Church as his words have been set to song for the Church. And, who was Jude? You may well ask. The name Jude is the shortened form of Judah and, though neither man speaks of it, Jude joins James as the half-brothers of Jesus! He had lived with them in Nazareth until they were grown men. Both disbelieved His true identity until the unmistakable proof of His resurrection was presented to them *personally*!

162. THE LORD IS ABLE
Jude, verses 24, 25. Tune: *Warrington* L.M.

The LORD is able to present
Us each within His presence: whole,
Without a fault, with greatest joy;
This is for us our utmost goal.

To Him, the only God, our King,
Be glory, majesty, and power,
Authority, through Christ our Lord
Who guards and guides us every hour.

Before all ages had begun,
And to this present time, our Lord
Has kept us ever in His care;
Now and fore'er we trust His word.

..... oOo .....

SCRIPTURE IN SONG

There are songs yet to be sung! Some of the most glorious are found in the pages of the **APOCALYPSE—REVELATION**—as told by **JOHN**. Jesus had said unequivocally: *No one knows the day or hour of My return.* He also said: *discern the seasons—observe the fig tree in spring, "see" what it "says"!* You see the fruit forming? The fruit is even now bourgeoning! This song tells of it.

163. THE LORD IS COMING SOON!
Revelation 1:1–8. Tune: *Toplady* 7.7.7.7.7.7.

Now to Him who loves us so,
And has freed us from our sins
By His Blood: He made us whole,
All to be His Kingdom priests:
He has bid us serve Him here;
"Glory!" echoes from the soul.

Look! the Lord is coming soon,
See the clouds disperse at noon!
Every eye shall see the Lord,
Even those who pierced Him through,
And all peoples of the Earth
Then shall mourn because of God.

Alpha and Omega, LORD,
He's the One who always *IS*,
First and Last, the One to come,
He is God with *Yahweh*, LORD:
Past and Present, Future: One!
El Shaddai, the Mighty God!

Amen, Amen, Amen, LORD,
Yahweh El Shaddai, LORD, God!
Glory to Your Holy Name,
All things flow at Your command!
Amen, Amen, Amen, LORD:
All creation will proclaim.

SCRIPTURE IN SONG

164. ETERNITY BEYOND TIME

Revelation–selected verses.   Tune: *Sweet Hour of Prayer*   D.L.M.

To Him who is and was, and yet
To come, and Jesus—Risen Lord
Who rules supreme—to Him be praise!
To Him who, by His precious blood,
From every sin has set us free
To serve within God's Holy Place
As Kingdom priests in righteousness:
To Him be glory, power, and praise.

How worthy is the Lamb once slain!
He will receive all power and wealth,
All wisdom, strength, and honour due:
All glory be to Him on Earth!
To Him who sits on Heaven's Throne
And to the Lamb of God, be praise;
All glory be to Jesus Christ;
Forever we'll extol His grace!

We'll stand before the Throne of God
And we shall hear His welcome there;
His Presence shall our Sanctuary be,
No more shall darkness cast its fear!
The Lamb of God shall shepherd us
And lead us to the Living Spring
Where thirst is quenched: He'll wipe our tears
And we will to His glory sing!

The ransomed host, cleansed by His blood,
Triumphant, sings the Lamb's own song:
How marvellous, Almighty God:
To You the glory shall belong!
How just and true are all Your ways,
Eternal King, the Holy One.
All nations come to worship You:
Your righteousness the vict'ry won!

EPILOGUE

165. THE BENEDICTION
Revelation 22:12–21
With Matthew 24:32–34, 25:32–34
Tune: *Diademata*   D.S.M.

Behold, I'm coming soon!
'Yes, Lord, Your promise stands.'
'The time is short, so be alert:
Each day is in your hands.
The hour is not yet known,
Though seasons are in place;
When buds are seen, the fruit is near!
Now realise God's peace.

'The Shepherd of your soul
Will come to you, enfold
You in the Heav'nly Pastures, where
All fear at last is quelled.
Unless the time be short,
All things would cease to be.
Discern the seasons, trust in Me:
And *LIVE* eternally.'

.....

'EVEN SO, COME LORD JESUS.'

THE GRACE OF JESUS, OUR LORD,
BE WITH YOU ALL. AMEN.

..... oOo .....